"This will be a tool I will put in the hands of one person after another. Will clearly and biblically addresses the questions that tend to haunt so many, and in so doing infuses us with hope, reminds us of our Father's grace, and causes us to smile."

Jeff Young, pastor of spiritual development,
Prestonwood Baptist Church, Plano, Texas

"Will Davis has nailed it. He has identified the most common lies that keep people from experiencing true freedom in Christ and has replaced them with the truth. I was in shock when I saw that some of those lies had crept into my own mind. Thank you, Will, for putting us all back on the solid ground of grace-filled truth!"

Tim Liston, senior pastor, New Hope Church,
Manvel, Texas

"We found ourselves smiling with relief as we read the pages of *10 Things Jesus Never Said*. With stunning simplicity, Will Davis diffuses debilitating, unfounded guilt, inviting us to enjoy God with newfound trust and empowering truth."

Bob and Audrey Meisner, television hosts, *It's a New Day*;
bestselling authors M— *over*

"Will Davis has a special at ... insights in a way that makes y ... on
a journey and knows exactly ... est
person alive who hasn't stru ... in
this book. The freedom you w ... you read may change your
life forever!"

Ryan Rush, senior pastor, Bannockburn Baptist Church,
Austin, Texas

"This is Will Davis Jr.'s best book yet. You are about to be humbled, dismantled, and brought face-to-face with the misbeliefs that have stood between you and the most beautiful love that has ever been known. Be ready to fall on your face and into his arms and feel the divine lightness of his cross on your shoulders. Know this love. Nothing else matters."

Nancy Turner, host, *This Is the Day*, Moody Radio

Other Books by Will Davis Jr.

Pray Big
Pray Big for Your Marriage
Pray Big for Your Child
Faith Set Free
Why Faith Makes Sense

10 THINGS **JESUS** NEVER SAID

and why you should **STOP** believing them

WILL DAVIS JR.

Revell

a division of Baker Publishing Group
Grand Rapids, Michigan

Published by Revell
a division of Baker Publishing Group
P.O. Box 6287, Grand Rapids, MI 49516-6287
www.revellbooks.com

Printed in the United States of America

Library of Congress Cataloging-in-Publication Data
Davis, Will, 1962–
     10 things Jesus never said : and why you should stop believing them / Will
   Davis, Jr.
        p.   cm.
     Includes bibliographical references (p.   ).
     ISBN 978-0-8007-2001-8 (pbk.)
     1. Christian life. 2. Jesus Christ—Teachings. I. Title. II. Title: Ten things
   Jesus never said.
   BV4501.3.D385 2011
   248.4—dc22   2011004368

Published in association with the literary agency of WordServe Literary Group, Ltd., 10152 S. Knoll Circle, Highlands Ranch, CO 80130.

To protect the privacy of those who have shared their stories with the author, some details and names have been changed. Any similarity to individuals the reader may know is coincidental.

11   12   13   14   15   16   17   7   6   5   4   3   2   1

To my friend Dave Busby,
who now lives in heaven.
He was the best example
of grace in action I've ever known.
Learn more about Dave at davebusby.com.

Contents

Contents

Acknowledgments

Thanks to . . .

Susie Davis—for repeatedly showing me unmerited grace.

Will, Emily, and Sara Davis—for understanding what matters.

Greg Johnson—for helping to make this book happen.

Vicki Crumpton, Deonne Beron, Janelle Mahlmann, Debbie Deacon, Claudia Marsh, Karen Steele, Dwight Baker, and the amazing team at Baker and Revell—it's a pleasure to be partnering with you.

The overseers, executive team, board of directors, and staff of Austin Christian Fellowship—for learning about grace with me and for encouraging me to write.

Joni Kendrick—for putting up with me, protecting me, rebuking me, and making me laugh.

Cordel and Christy Robinson—for defying the odds.

Peter Larkam—for modeling biblical forgiveness.

Audrey and Bob Meisner—for sharing your story and helping heal countless broken marriages.

Randy and Denise Phillips—I love you both. Randy, are you ready to get saved?

Terri Crow—for another round of impeccable proofreading. You're the best.

Introduction

What would happen if you were invited to a face-to-face meeting with Jesus? Suppose it was just you and Jesus for an hour, sitting directly across from each other, so close your knees were almost touching. What do you think he would say? Would you be uncomfortable? Would you look forward to that meeting? Would you eagerly jump at the chance to spend an hour with the incarnate God? Or would you dread it? What would you do if you were told to spend an hour alone with Jesus?

For many, spending any time alone with Jesus sounds absolutely wonderful. They know that someday they will be in his presence, and they eagerly look forward to their unbroken fellowship with him. But for many others, unfortunately, such an invitation doesn't sound too inviting. It's not that they don't love Jesus and long to finally and fully be in his presence; it's just that many of them—or I should say *us*—live with a tremendous sense of guilt in their respective Christian walks. They know they don't measure up to God's high and holy standards. They believe they are constantly letting Jesus down, embarrassing him, and even causing him pain. If you felt like that about someone—a boss, a parent, a spouse, or a friend—would you look forward to spending time with him or her? Probably not.

So what do you think Jesus would say to you? How would the conversation start? I've asked that question to adults and teenagers all over the country. The answers are typically something like these:

I'm so disappointed in you.

What were you thinking?

You are a serious letdown.

You have no idea the damage you've done to my reputation.

If you were really a Christian, you wouldn't act like you do.

If you really loved me, you'd try harder.

We're done.

And one of my personal favorites: *I'm really getting tired of forgiving the same old sin.*

For a group of people supposedly saved by grace, loved unconditionally, and secure in our relationship with Christ, we certainly carry a lot of guilt and baggage in our relationship with God. Our hearts and minds are filled with tapes that play over and over, and the messages aren't very inspiring. *You don't measure up. You're not doing enough. I can't believe you call yourself a Christian.*

The problem is that many of the things we believe Jesus would say to us are actually things he never said and never would say. They're patently unbiblical and don't represent the heart of Christ. As Holy Spirit–sealed followers of Jesus, we must learn to push back against the mental messages that tell us how fed up with us God is. We must bring those rogue thoughts under the authority of our loving Lord Jesus. We need to rethink our theology and let God's revealed truth direct our beliefs about him, not some fictitious statement that doesn't even come close to accurately representing how Jesus feels about us. In short, we need to reject the things Jesus didn't say and start believing the things he did.

In the chapters that follow, I will unmask several commonly believed myths about our relationship with God. I will expose many of the things that we think Jesus would say to us if he had the chance, and compare them to what he actually said. Then I want to replace the terrible failed theology of condemnation that so many of us have with the truth of how Jesus really feels about us. When you're done reading this book, I hope you will be much more confident, emboldened, and joyful in your relationship with God.

But before we look at what Jesus didn't say, we need to examine something he did say. In fact, I believe it may be the most important thing he ever said. By doing so, we'll not only gain great hope and assurance of how he feels about us, but we'll also lay the foundation for refuting the things he actually never said.

PART 1

THE MOST IMPORTANT THING JESUS EVER SAID

1

I Will Give You Rest

On July 4, 2010, I decided to celebrate our nation's birthday by doing a long and difficult solo mountain climb. I hiked to the summit of a mountain I've climbed many times before—Mt. Ypsilon. But this time, instead of taking the gentle western slopes to the thirteen-thousand-foot summit, I took a much more difficult route. It's called Donner Ridge. The final three miles of the push to the summit up Donner Ridge are considered Class 3. That means the route is extremely steep and requires much hand-to-foot scrambling. Class 3 climbs are just below technical. (Technical climbs are Class 4—they require ropes, helmets, carabiners, and harnesses. Class 3 climbs require you to be just a little crazy.) I found that Donner Ridge was every bit a Class 3 and then some.

It was, quite honestly, one of the most demanding physical things I've ever done. There was no trail and no way markers, and I didn't see another person the entire time I was on the ridge. Since I was hiking alone, I obviously had to be extra careful. If I were to step off into a deep hole, no one would ever know.

But I made it. After several hours of extremely strenuous climbing, I reached the summit of Mt. Ypsilon via Donner Ridge. My climb took so long that I spent literally only a few minutes on the top. Thunderstorms were brewing all around me, so I made a quick exit to the nearest tree line. (In the opposite direction, I might add, of the trailhead and my car!)

While on the ridge, I made a critical decision that I'm sure helped me not only survive the climb but also reach the summit. I decided to rest. On a long, hard climb, sometimes the most important time on the mountain is the time you spend not doing anything. Those brief minutes of rest give your body the necessary breathing time to catch up with your exertion level; they give you time to take in some much-needed food and water; and they allow you to enjoy the view, mark your progress, and remember why you started up the mountain in the first place.

Rest on a long, difficult journey is vital.

That's why I believe that one of the most important statements Jesus ever made was about rest. To a group of road-weary spiritual seekers, Jesus said, "Come to me, all you who are weary and burdened, and I will give you rest. Take my yoke upon you and learn from me, for I am gentle and humble in heart, and you will find rest for your souls. For my yoke is easy and my burden is light" (Matt. 11:28–30). Have you ever heard more beautiful or inviting words? Against the backdrop of a culture that stressed the importance of religious performance, Jesus invited hungry souls to rest. He basically said, "Hey, if you're worn out from trying to keep all the rules and making sure that you're pleasing God enough, why don't you just come to me? I'll do the work for you."

Those words must have sounded really good to all the spiritual dropouts who had found the demands of keeping their cultural and religious laws to be too rigorous—or rather, impossible. Those words must have also reverberated through the religious establishment, whose members had cut their spiritual teeth believing that God indeed kept score and they didn't want to end up on the short side of his ledger. Many of the religious leaders of Jesus' day, however noble their intentions may have been, believed and taught that God was best appeased by painstaking adherence to hundreds and hundreds of rules and regulations. A few brave souls found comfort in believing they could manage or dictate their status before God by trying to keep the rules. Most just found exhaustion.

And then Jesus came along and offered rest. Specifically, he offered rest through a relationship with him. Let's consider what he said.

Jesus' Invitation: Come to Me

I've always found it curious that Jesus constantly invited people to himself. Today we invite people to church, a small group, a conference, or a special event. We invite them to read a book, watch a DVD, or listen to a message. But we always invite people who are hungry for spiritual truth to pursue or investigate something other than ourselves. We say, "This is what you need," or, "Truth can be found here." Imagine what kind of crazy looks you would get if you told your spiritually inquisitive friends that all they needed to do to discover truth was to come and be with you, that you were somehow what they were looking for. Hopefully, you know better.

Not Jesus. He didn't hesitate to tell people that what their souls most desperately needed could be found solely in a relationship with him. He didn't point to a philosophy, a religion, or a place of worship. He tapped himself on his chest and said, "I am what you're looking for." To the seekers of purpose, meaning, and truth, Jesus said that he himself was the end of their search:

> "The Spirit of the Lord is on me, because he has anointed me to preach good news to the poor. He has sent me to proclaim freedom for the prisoners and recovery of sight for the blind, to release the oppressed, to proclaim the year of the Lord's favor" (Luke 4:18–19).

> "I tell you the truth, whoever hears my word and believes him who sent me has eternal life and will not be condemned; he has crossed over from death to life" (John 5:24).

> "I am the bread of life. He who comes to me will never go hungry, and he who believes in me will never be thirsty" (John 6:35).

> "If anyone is thirsty, let him come to me and drink. Whoever believes in me, as the Scripture has said, streams of living water will flow from within him" (John 7:37–38).

> "I am the light of the world. Whoever follows me will never walk in darkness, but will have the light of life" (John 8:12).

> "I am the resurrection and the life. He who believes in me will live, even though he dies; and whoever lives and believes in me will never die" (John 11:25–26).

"You call me 'Teacher' and 'Lord,' and rightly so, for that is what I am" (John 13:13).

Do you see a theme developing here? Either Jesus was the most self-centered, self-deluded person in history, or he was indeed the answer to every human's prayers and the fulfillment of every hungry soul's dreams.

When you enter into a relationship with Jesus, you are not entering into a system that is maintained by your hard work, or one where you will be graded for your performance. You are not told to obey the rules, check off the boxes, or keep a running tally of your deeds. You're simply invited to know him.

Jesus' Guest List: All You Who Are Weary and Burdened

Jesus didn't target the put-together, the well-polished, and the religious performers. Chances are they wouldn't have seen their need for what he offered anyway. Rather, Jesus targeted the down-and-out, the spiritually bankrupt, and the religiously lost. All those who didn't seem to make the cut or who couldn't meet the impossibly high standards set by the religious elite were the very ones Jesus invited to come to him.

Notice how he described them—"weary and burdened." Our initial reaction when hearing that is to think about physical exhaustion. I think of a traveler in Jesus' day after a day of walking, or a merchant carrying a heavy load to market, or a farmer who has spent a day working in the heat of the sun—or me about two-thirds of the way up Donner Ridge. Any of those could well be described as weary and burdened. But Jesus obviously had more in mind than just physical exhaustion. He was speaking of spiritual exhaustion.

The weary and burdened Jesus referred to are those who realize the futility of their efforts to appease God. Consider Tracy. She is thirty-seven, never married, and struggles with chronic depression. Tracy had a difficult childhood with an overbearing father and an absent mother. She has attempted suicide twice and is on various medications for her mental and emotional struggles. Tracy is also a Christ-follower, but she never feels like she can please God. In her eyes, her life is a royal mess and she has very little to offer God. She feels like she is a constant letdown to him, and that no matter how hard she tries, no matter how much she prays or serves, her emotional struggles always trump her ability to please her heavenly Father.

It is to people like Tracy that Jesus offered this invitation. Not just those with obvious emotional or mental battles, but also those who feel completely frustrated in their efforts to make God happy. If you feel like you're always a day late and a dollar short in your relationship with God, or if you feel like you will never be able to do enough to get into his good graces, then Jesus was talking to you.

In his teaching in Matthew 11:28–30, Jesus used a familiar image from his day to help his audience understand what he was offering them: "Take my yoke upon you. . . . For my yoke is easy and my burden is light." Farmers knew all about yokes—those heavy wooden and leather harnesses that fit over the head and shoulders of oxen. They kept the oxen pulling together in the same direction.

No doubt many in Jesus' audience could identify with the heavy yoke of their cultural and religious legal code. The countless rules and regulations were impossible to keep up with, much less adhere to. So Jesus offered his yoke instead. He taught and modeled a faith system that was based on grace, forgiveness, and healing. He said that if weary spiritual seekers would join themselves to him, they would actually find joy and abundant life in the process, not spiritual burnout.

For someone like Tracy, Jesus' words couldn't be any sweeter: "Connect yourself to me and let me do the work. I'll make you pure, I'll heal your wounds, and I'll make you right before God." If you have ever found yourself at the end of your proverbial rope, especially in your efforts to measure up before a holy God, then know that you are exactly the kind of person Jesus had in mind when he made this offer. You're on his guest list.

Jesus' Promise: I Will Give You Rest

In the months following the miraculous exodus of the Israelites from their captivity in Egypt, Moses found himself in an unlikely and unenviable position. As he led the people through the wilderness, they constantly moaned and complained about how bad things were for them. They had quickly forgotten how much they had suffered in Egypt and dared to gripe about their living conditions after God had led them out of slavery. On more than one occasion God offered or threatened to wipe out the entire ungrateful bunch and start over with Moses and a new nation. Moses often ended up pleading to God for mercy and patience with the rebellious and ungrateful Israelites.

In one poignant moment, Moses pleaded for God to protect the people and continue to guide them. He then prayed, "If you are pleased with me, teach me your ways so I may know you and continue to find favor with you. Remember that this nation is your people" (Exod. 33:13). That's quite a daring prayer. Moses boldly asked God not just to grant favor to his rebellious people but also to grant it to him as their leader. He prayed that God might take him on as his very own student. I envy Moses' boldness before God and must confess that I have prayed this prayer for myself on many occasions.

God's response to Moses was far beyond anything Moses may have hoped for: "The LORD replied, 'My Presence will go with you, and I will give you rest'" (Exod. 33:14). The promise of God's presence must have been music to the ears of Moses and his wandering people. God wasn't obligated to just hang out with them. If he chose to abandon them, they'd be sitting ducks for the marauding nations that inhabited the lands around them. The promise of God's presence brought with it the guarantee of his provision and protection for his people. Moses must have been humbled and thrilled.

But it's the second part of God's promise to Moses that really merits our interest here: "I will give you rest." This latter promise is the result of the former: "Because my presence will be with you, because you'll know my protection and provision, you'll have rest." There's a cause-and-effect relationship here: God's presence yields God's rest. The Hebrews knew that by *rest*, God meant not only the protection of their boundaries from invading hordes but also the emotional, mental, and spiritual confidence they would have knowing that God was irreversibly with them. *Rest* meant that they could stop worrying about what might happen tomorrow and what enemy might be waiting for them around the next corner. And don't overlook this point: *rest* was inseparable from God's presence. One always accompanies the other.

Now let's jump from Exodus to Matthew in the Bible, about 1,400 years later. Jesus stood before a group of weary spiritual seekers and invited them to enter into a relationship with him. What did he promise? "I will give you rest." That was no accidental statement by Jesus. Any good Hebrew knew what God had promised Moses and the Israelites back in Exodus. Those words were some of the sweetest ever spoken by God to a person or a people. So when Jesus said them, he fully understood the implications of what he was saying.

Imagine the murmur that must have moved through the crowd as listeners turned to each other and said, "Did he just say what I think he said?" No one, and I mean NO ONE, quoted God as an equal and lived to tell about it. When Jesus invoked the "I will give you rest" promise, he was saying that he had the same ability to bring peace, protection, and provision to people's lives as did the God who'd spoken to Moses in Exodus. He was saying they were one and the same—that his presence was the same as God's presence, and his rest the same as God's rest.

Setting aside the obvious theological implications of Jesus' statement for just a minute, let's think about the implications for our lives and faith. In his invitation to road-weary spiritual seekers, Jesus offered to be to them what God was to the nation of Israel while they wandered in the desert. He promised to those who followed him that he would be their shelter, defender, leader, and provider. And with those things would come the mental, emotional, and spiritual rest that can occur only when a person knows with absolute certainty that God is his or her advocate, not an adversary.

What's the Point?

What we do together right now is extremely important, so you might want to put the book down and stretch or grab a cup of coffee before you finish this chapter. What we learn together right here and now will become the platform from which we refute the ten lies that so many of us believe about Jesus and how he feels about us.

Are you ready? Here we go.

We can draw at least two profound conclusions from Jesus' invitation in Matthew 11:28 that should forever mark how we view and understand our relationship with him.

Jesus Wants You

Make no mistake about it—Jesus extended his holy invitation for rest to *you*. You are not the grand exception in history that God cannot or will not love. You have not gone so far that he can't or won't forgive you. When Jesus spoke this invitation, he didn't aim it just at the really good people or the really pretty people or the really churchy people. He aimed it at the spiritually broken. If you find yourself nearing the end of your rope spiritually, if you find your stamina and desire to keep trying to earn God's favor rapidly waning, then you're exactly the kind of person Jesus was reaching out to. If you're not spiritually worn out or if you somehow think you have it all together, then you probably won't get anything out of reading this book. Just keep on going like you have been. Chances are, brokenness will find you. But if you feel desperate before God and yet hopeless without him, then you're exactly where God wants you.

Here's a little exercise. I want you to make Jesus' invitation personal. You know that he said, "Come to me, all you who are weary." The adjective *all* has a powerful meaning there, signifying that there are no limits about whom Jesus is willing to receive. But the broadness of the comment can still leave some feeling left out or wondering if it really applies to them. So let's narrow it down. Here's the statement again, with a minor change: "Come to me, _____, and I will give you rest." I want you to write your name in that blank, and I want you to do it right now. Then read it out loud a few times. Let God's Spirit speak it to you.

Come to me, *Tony*. Come to me, *Sandy*. Come to me, *Amanda*. Come to me, *Carlos*. Come to me, *Benjamin*. Come to me, *Ajid*. Come to me, *Trevor*. Come to me, *Russ*. Come to me, *Mohammed*. Come to me, *Sylvia*. Come to me, *Will*. Come to me, _____.

We could spend the rest of our lives filling in the blanks, because the beautiful and undeniable biblical reality is that the invitation is for every one of us. Including *you*.

Whatever the Size of Your Burden, Jesus Wants It

Jesus is in the business of burden lifting. Part of his mission is to remove the load from the shoulders of religious seekers and weary spiritual travelers. It doesn't matter what the load is, how long you've carried it, or how ugly it might be. If it's weighing you down and sapping your spiritual strength, Jesus wants it.

Let me be specific:

You were abused as a child. You have trouble trusting others and forgiving. *Jesus wants your burden.*

You recently had an affair and have terribly wounded the people you love most in the world. *Jesus wants your burden.*

27

You've had massive financial failures and had to file bankruptcy. *Jesus wants your burden.*

You struggle with contentment. *Jesus wants your burden.*

You often feel afraid. *Jesus wants your burden.*

You're a worrier. *Jesus wants your burden.*

You have always struggled with your weight. You don't feel attractive to others. *Jesus wants your burden.*

You feel consumed by guilt. *Jesus wants your burden.*

You hate your life and wish you could start over. *Jesus wants your burden.*

You battle depression. *Jesus wants your burden.*

You're a recovering drug addict or alcoholic. *Jesus wants your burden.*

You have a gambling addiction. *Jesus wants your burden.*

You secretly look at pornography. *Jesus wants your burden.*

You have never felt significant. You always feel like the world is passing you by. *Jesus wants your burden.*

You're lonely. *Jesus wants your burden.*

You feel like God is always angry with you. *Jesus wants your burden.*

You feel like you're always letting God down. *Jesus wants your burden.*

You don't think you can ever be good enough for God. *Jesus wants your burden.*

You _____ (write your burden in the blank). *Jesus wants your burden.*

There is no statute of limitations for the burdens that Jesus is willing to take. It doesn't matter how long-standing the burden is, how weighty, how distasteful, or how intimidating. Whatever your burden is, he wants it.

Come to Me, All You Who Are Weary and Burdened

At the end of every chapter and at the end of the book, we'll come back to this invitation from Jesus. I want to keep it fresh for you. It represents the heart of what he has said to us. It's his red-letter teaching summed up in one beautiful sentence.

But first we have some work to do. Now that we know what Jesus has said and how he really feels about us, we are ready to take on the lies that so many of us believe about God and our relationship with him. We're ready to expose and refute the things Jesus *didn't* say. So let's get to it. There's great news ahead.

Small Group Discussion Questions

1. Why did you choose to read this book? What need of yours do you hope it will address?
2. Think about the opening question in the introduction. If you were asked to sit face-to-face with Jesus, what would happen? What do you think he would say?
3. In what part of your relationship with God do you most need to expose the lies of what Jesus didn't say and embrace the truth of what he did say?
4. Read Matthew 11:28–30 out loud. As you listen, imagine that Jesus is speaking these words directly to you: "Come to me, all you who are weary and burdened, and I will give you rest. Take my yoke upon you and learn from me, for I am gentle and humble in heart, and you will find rest for your souls. For my yoke is easy and my burden is light." How did you feel as you listened? What burden would you most like for Jesus to take from you today?
5. In your own words, define *rest*—not the rest you feel after a good night's sleep, but the kind of rest promised by Jesus. What does that look like in today's world?
6. What's involved in learning to stay yoked to Jesus? How can we keep from slipping back into the rut of carrying our own burdens?
7. After reading this chapter, how will you live differently?

PART 2

THINGS JESUS
NEVER SAID

2

You're Too Far Gone to Be Saved

Is there ever a point where we get too sinful for God? If we hit new moral lows or set records in the sin department, isn't there a line we cross where we simply move beyond God's reach? Wouldn't God be wise to say that there are just certain things he won't forgive?

After all, in the world God created, there are clearly points of no return. If someone commits a heinous crime, they can go to jail or, in some cases, even forfeit their life for what they did. For some extremely poor decisions, there's only justice and consequences. Why wouldn't it be the same with God? Why shouldn't we expect that God, who is fair and just, would determine that there are just certain things he won't pardon? Why wouldn't we expect God to say, "Hey, you did this, now you've got to live with it"? Is there a point where we're simply too sinful for God to save?

Consider Amanda. Amanda is a beautiful twentysomething who attends our church. She is single and has always tried to honor God. Recently Amanda came to me after a service. She was a broken young woman and could barely look me in the eye. "I've done something terrible," she said. "I'm in a relationship with a guy, and I've done something I never thought I'd do. I gave him something I shouldn't have, and I know I can never get it back. I'm so ashamed. I'm fearful now that God won't have me. I think I'm too dirty, too sinful. . . ." Her words dissolved in tears.

Amanda's story is a familiar one. Most of us know what it's like to wonder if we've strayed so far or sinned so grievously that we can no longer be forgiven. For some, like Amanda, it's lost purity. For others, it's an affair, a felony, or a multiyear secret sin. But whatever the issue, the result is the same—we seriously doubt if God can still save us.

The Lie

Jesus certainly didn't die for the likes of you. You may have friends or family who are Christians, but they never messed up like you have. You're crazy to think that God still wants you. You're damaged goods. You've gone too far. How dare you think that God might still be willing to forgive you! How arrogant can you be? He gave you one chance after another, and now that you've blown it royally, you think he's just going to forgive everything and call it even? No way. He's done with you. There are just some sins God won't forgive. There are just some people he won't ever pardon. And guess what—you're one of them.

Have you ever heard something like that? I've talked to adults and teenagers all over the nation who have heard some form of those very words. Sometimes they hear them from others, but most frequently they hear them from themselves. They've convinced themselves that they're disqualified. They want to follow Christ, they want to seek forgiveness, but they really believe they've gone too far. They feel like they're hopelessly lost in their sin.

But they're not, and neither are you. No one is ever too dirty or too sinful for God to save them.

The Truth

The biblical reality is that as long as you're still drawing breath, you can be saved. The only point of no return when it comes to salvation is death. Before that, we're all still candidates for God's grace—no exceptions. No person in history has ever been ineligible for salvation, no matter how evil he or she may have been. Regardless of what your guilty conscience or the devil may be whispering in your ear, the reality is that God loves you and is ready and willing to grant you salvation right now. Let me show you two reasons why.

God Doesn't Grade on a Curve

We want to categorize sin. We see sin in levels. You know—little sins, big sins, really bad sins, and so on. We think the people with really bad sins are much worse than those with little sins, and we expect God to treat us accordingly. We expect God to feel differently about those who sin a lot than he does about those who sin just a little. The problem with such thinking is that it isn't biblical.

In the book of James, Jesus' half brother wrote, "For whoever keeps the whole law and yet stumbles at just one point is

35

guilty of breaking all of it. For he who said, 'Do not commit adultery,' also said, 'Do not murder.' If you do not commit adultery but do commit murder, you have become a law-breaker" (James 2:10–11). His point? There are no divisions in sin. A guy who only tells lies is as guilty as a guy who commits murder, and a girl who sins only a few times a day (if that is even possible) is the same as one who sins hundreds of times a day. All sin is ultimately the same in God's eyes, and when it comes to our need for God's grace and forgiveness, we're all in the same boat.

That being true, no one is ever out of God's reach. He doesn't see people as murderers or liars or adulterers or terrorists. He sees them as sinners. And every last one of them is eligible for his salvation, no matter what they've done. Including you.

God Treats the Disease of Sin, Not Its Symptoms

As I'm writing these words, I'm battling a cold. Nothing too serious—just enough to put me in a foul mood. I'm in the second day of it, and I'm dealing with a different set of symptoms. Yesterday I had a runny nose and a sore throat. Today I have a cough and a headache. Tomorrow? I can't wait to find out. The point is that the source is the same—my cold—but the symptoms are different.

Sin is like that. It will manifest different symptoms in people, but the root issue is always the same. You could easily name some notorious sinners from history right now, people known for their terrible acts against humanity—mass murderers, assassins, dictators. Each manifested his or her evil in different ways, but each still had the same problem—sin. Different symptoms but the same disease. And those famous sinners had the same disease as some of the noblest people who have ever lived. Think of heroic Christian leaders over the centuries—John Wesley, Martin Luther, Hudson Taylor, Mother Teresa. Each had the same disease as the notorious sinners, but the symptoms were different.

Note this, however: just because a sin doesn't make headlines or land a person in jail doesn't mean it's any less serious. Sinful acts are the fruit of a broken, sin-filled heart. And that's what God deals with in each of us—our sinful hearts.

In Psalm 51, David talked about his own sin disease: "For I know my transgressions, and my sin is always before me. Against you, you only, have I sinned and done what is evil in your sight, so that you are proved right when you speak and justified when you judge. Surely I was sinful at birth, sinful from the time my mother conceived me" (vv. 3–5). In this brutal confession by the man after God's own heart, David acknowledged the root of his troubles. He understood that he was guilty not for what he had done but simply for who he was.

David certainly could have listed off several "big" sins—stuff like adultery, murder, conspiracy, and lying. Those are the types of sins that we think just might make a person unsalvageable to God. But David didn't dwell on his sin's symptoms. He simply confessed that he was born guilty. The only thing David's specific sins did was make the case that he, like you and me, was guilty before God and desperately needed grace.

God doesn't see sins, he sees the sinner. He doesn't see a murderer, a liar, a gossip, a slanderer, a drug addict, or a lazy person. He sees people in need of grace. And he sent his Son into the world to deal with the root cause of our symptoms—sin.

Exhibit A

Consider the woman caught in the act of adultery. John tells us her story in chapter 8 of his Gospel:

> Jesus went to the Mount of Olives. At dawn he appeared again in the temple courts, where all the people gathered around him, and he sat down to teach them. The teachers of the law and the Pharisees brought in a woman caught in adultery. They made her stand before the group and said to Jesus, "Teacher, this woman was caught in the act of adultery. In the Law Moses commanded us to stone such women. Now what do you say?" (John 8:1–5)

Scholars have long wondered why the Pharisees didn't bring the man in as well. Adultery is a couple's offense. Since the woman had been caught in the very act, where was her partner? Perhaps he escaped. Or perhaps he was standing alongside his fellow Pharisees, only now as one of the woman's accusers.

The law of Moses indeed called for the execution of those guilty of adultery. As there were apparently dozens of eyewitnesses to her crime, this woman was a candidate for death. If Jesus agreed with the mob and condoned her execution, then his message of grace and forgiveness would be shattered. He would be endorsing the very religious tactics that he seemed determined to resist. But if Jesus pardoned her, then he wouldn't be keeping the law that he claimed to love and support. It appeared to be the ultimate catch-22 for Jesus. Either way he would lose.

Jesus' response to the scene has always moved me. He simply knelt down and began to doodle in the dirt on the temple floor. Some have speculated that there was something significant to what he wrote in the dirt. If there was, John didn't tell us. What we do know is that as Jesus knelt down and began to write, the mob and those in the temple crowd directed their attention to Jesus. The longer he doodled, the more they focused on him.

Soon the mob began yelling at Jesus to give them an answer. They thought he was stalling. He wasn't. He was taking all the attention off the woman.

Amazingly, in that critical moment when Jesus was being tested by his enemies, he was thinking about this adulterous woman. *How must she feel, standing there naked and exposed in her sin? What fears must she have, knowing that the stones of judgment might begin falling on her at any moment?* If Jesus could have ever justified casting off a sinner, she was the one. Hers was an open-and-shut case. But Jesus didn't cast her off, and he didn't condemn her. He knelt and pulled all the attention away from her, and by doing so he showed just how much he cares for struggling sinners.

You probably know how the story ends. Jesus masterfully defused the situation by telling the Pharisees that if any of them were sinless, they could start the stoning. They all knew better, as did the crowd watching them. They filed out, defeated and deflated, leaving the woman alone before Jesus. Let's let John conclude the scene for us:

> Jesus straightened up and asked her, "Woman, where are they? Has no one condemned you?"
>
> "No one, sir," she said.
>
> "Then neither do I condemn you," Jesus declared. "Go now and leave your life of sin." (John 8:10–11)

What sweet words to us fallen sinners—"Neither do I condemn you. Go now and leave your life of sin." Can you go too far from God to be forgiven? No. This is the Savior who doesn't chase away sinners but chases after them.

Jesus on Bourbon Street

I met Larry Broussard not long after his thirty-eighth birthday. He had been a Christ-follower for only a few weeks. He was also a former homosexual, a recovering alcoholic and cocaine addict, and HIV-positive. I was twenty-five years old and the pastor of a small Baptist church in north Austin. When I reached for my seminary text explaining how to connect "people like Larry" with "people like Baptists," I found my bookshelf empty. The year was 1987, and the AIDS virus was still a mystery to many. Doctors still weren't quite sure how the virus was transmitted. As a result, much fear and confusion hovered around the disease.

The church I served was a sweet and relatively healthy Southern Baptist congregation. We prided ourselves on being welcoming to all and open-minded about the new challenges God would bring us. However, the idea of a formerly gay guy with AIDS serving as a greeter, singing in the choir, or being a sponsor at youth camp . . . well, let's just say it stretched the limits of open-mindedness for some of our more con-servative members.

In my efforts to guide Larry safely into the fellowship of our church without either of us being lynched, I got to spend a lot of time with him. He was one of the most remarkable people I've ever known, and I am grateful to God for bring-ing him into the path of my ministry. He was one of the best things that ever happened to our little church. His story is nothing short of amazing.

When Larry was thirteen, a minister in the church that his family attended molested him. The encounter left him convinced that not only was he gay but he was also a religious misfit. As a young teenager, Larry wrote off any chance of ever having a meaningful relationship with a church or, more importantly, God. He threw himself into the sport of dance—an area in which he was naturally gifted—and into the party scene. Both soon came to dominate his life. In fact, Larry was a two-time world-champion ballroom dancer. In the sport of competitive ballroom dancing, he was an international celebrity.

In February of 1987, Larry and his friends made their annual trek to New Orleans for the Mardi Gras celebration. When you live for the party, Mardi Gras is a required stop on the tour. Larry remembered very little about his first few days in New Orleans. He was drunk and/or high the entire time. He also had numerous sexual encounters with several different men and women, most of whom he did not know. Larry wouldn't have labeled such behavior as extreme; it was how he lived. He moved from place to place, event to event, party to party, person to person, drug to drug, looking to meet the needs of his soul.

On one of the final nights of Mardi Gras, Larry and some of his friends were out looking for action on Bourbon Street. Larry saw a group of people walking their direction on the other side of the street. He immediately knew they weren't your typical Mardi Gras revelers. He quickly identified them as a group of Christians, the kind notorious for roaming the streets of the French Quarter, preaching hell and judgment and basically trying to ruin everyone else's fun. He could tell they were Christians because they were singing hymns, carrying Bibles, and led by some guy carrying a cross.

Larry snapped. He had been the object of more abuse and ridicule at the hands of "Christians" than he cared to remember. He felt that this group was somehow hostile toward him personally and invading his space. So he left his friends and boldly marched across the street to confront the would-be evangelists. He verbally lashed out at them for their judgmental attitudes and hypocrisy. He used every derogatory word he knew to vent the pain and humiliation he'd felt toward the church for over two decades. But he didn't get the fight he expected. This group of Christians seemed, if anything, almost empathetic.

Larry's encounter with this group of Christians (who, by the way, were part of a mission group from Chillicothe, Missouri) lasted over three hours. It ended with Larry kneeling on Bourbon Street, in the midst of a wild Mardi Gras celebration, and asking Jesus to forgive his sins and to come into his tattered life. Larry showed up in my church office a month later. He was baptized and warmly received into our fellowship.

A year later, Larry's AIDS kicked in. He was diagnosed with lymphoma, a nasty side effect of having no immune system. Larry literally began to deteriorate before our eyes. Once strong and robust, he became gaunt, frail, and weak. His hair fell out from the chemo treatments. He was sick almost all the time, either from the intense treatments or from the lymphoma. Our church cared for Larry, and several members nursed him as if he were part of their family. But it was breaking our hearts to watch him die.

During that time, Larry never got angry with God over his disease. He wasn't a victim. He knew that he was reaping the consequences of choices he had made in his life before accepting Christ. He was, if anything, thankful for the chance to live out his final days in Christian community.

I'll never forget the day I was called to Seton Hospital in Austin. Larry was in a coma. To me, he looked dead already. It was so hard to see him that way. I said a prayer over Larry, hugged his grieving parents, and then left the bedside of one of the most authentic Christ-followers I'd ever known.

Then Larry woke up. And then he got up. And then he went home from the hospital. Larry's lymphoma had "mysteriously" gone into remission. Not only had he not died, he had made one of the most amazing comebacks from late-stage lymphoma that his doctors had ever seen.

In the next year of Larry's life, he traveled the world trying to rekindle some of his old friendships from his partying days. He received two lifetime achievement awards from his peers in the ballroom-dance community. At both awards ceremonies, Larry told the story of how Jesus had found him on the streets of New Orleans, how Jesus had forgiven his sins, and how Jesus had given him extra time to tell his friends about God's goodness. That he did with abandon.

Larry eventually moved to Houston to be closer to his parents. Up until the time that the AIDS virus finally took his life, Larry was active in his church, where he led a Bible study for men who were trying to break out of the homosexual lifestyle. When Larry died, he was free from any alcohol or drug use, and he was celibate. He had lived that way every day since he had heard about Jesus, years before, on Bourbon Street.

There's one more detail that makes Larry's story even more astounding. In February of 1988, instead of making his annual trek to New Orleans, Larry started a new tradition. He traveled to Chillicothe to celebrate the anniversary of his conversion to Christianity with the people who had introduced him to Jesus. They laughed, cried, and prayed together as they remembered that night a year before. During the conversation, one of the group's members asked Larry how he had known they were Christians.

Larry's response was immediate: "It was that guy with the cross. The minute I saw the man with the cross in front of your group, I knew who and what you were. That's what caught my attention—it was that crazy guy carrying the cross."

The group looked stunned. They were dead silent.

"What's the matter? Why are you all looking at me like that?" Larry asked.

Someone from the group responded, "Larry, what are you talking about? You're not making any sense. We didn't have any crosses. No one in our group was carrying a cross."

Larry pushed back. "You guys must have forgotten. There was someone, one of you, right in the front of your group carrying a huge cross. I remember thinking how stupid and out of place a cross looked on Bourbon Street. Come on, guys, you're starting to freak me out. Don't you remember the guy with the cross?"

"No, we don't," someone answered. "We didn't have anybody with a cross. Maybe there was a man carrying a cross who wasn't part of our group. Maybe you saw him and just came up to us instead."

Larry was starting to feel a little strange. "No, that's not what happened. I'm sure of it. I knew you guys were Christians because there was a man leading your group who was carrying a cross. I walked right by him to get to you. He was with your group. Look, I know I was high, but I wasn't hallucinating. I saw a man carrying a cross. He was in your group. That's how I knew you were Christians."

I don't know what Larry saw that night on Bourbon Street— an angel, a vision, Jesus himself? But I do know that the Jesus whom Larry heard about was real enough to free him in one miraculous instant from sexual, alcohol, and drug addictions. He was real enough to heal decades of pain, rejection, and unforgiveness. And he was real enough to give Larry a reason to live that he'd never known before.

Larry's story is proof to me that God will go anywhere, at any time, to love and rescue anyone, regardless of their sin. He is the God who pursues sinners, no matter how far they've fallen.

Come to Me, All You Who Are Weary and Burdened

What is the yoke of sin that you're carrying? What shame and guilt from transgressions past or present are keeping you from knowing God's love? You haven't gone too far. You may indeed be dirty, covered with sin—in reality, we all are—but you're not too dirty. No one is. God knew what he was getting into when he sent Jesus to redeem sinners. He didn't set preconditions for who was salvageable and who wasn't. He didn't set a limit on the size or scope of the iniquities that he was willing to pardon. He just sent Jesus to save sinners, and that covers us all.

You and all those you love are still candidates for God's mercy. You can turn to him in faith today and be saved and forgiven for all your sins—no limits, no exceptions. You are, right now, under the umbrella of his boundless love. Bring your sins to Jesus today and learn "together with all the saints . . . how wide and long and high and deep is the love of Christ, and to know this love that surpasses knowledge" (Eph. 3:18–19).

Small Group Discussion Questions

1. Did you ever feel that you were too far from God to be saved? Have you ever known anyone who felt that way? Have you ever worried about someone you love being too far gone for God to save? If so, can you give an example?

2. What's behind the thinking that certain people can't be forgiven? What cultural, religious, legal, or moral reasons do we have for thinking that some sinners just can't be saved? How do those differ from what the Bible teaches?

3. What's the most radical example of conversion you've ever seen? In other words, who do you know to be a Christian now, when you never thought they would be?

4. Read James 2:10–11. Why is someone who breaks only a small part of God's law as guilty as someone who breaks all of it?

5. Read Psalm 51:1–7. What do David's confessions and prayers tell you about sin, its origins in us, and how we can be forgiven?

6. Summarize Larry's story from the "Jesus on Bourbon Street" section. Have you ever known anyone like Larry? How did you feel as you read his story? What does Larry's story teach us about how far God is willing to go to reach a sinner?

7. After reading this chapter, do you feel more confident in the biblical teaching that no one is beyond saving? If so, how will that confidence impact how you view yourself and others? If not, what are you still struggling with?

8. After reading this chapter, how will you live differently?

3

I'm So Disappointed in You

My hometown of Austin, Texas, is surrounded by a beautiful series of lakes and rivers that are part of the charm of the Central Texas Hill Country. One of those lakes, Lady Bird Lake—named in honor of Lady Bird Johnson, former First Lady—cuts right through the heart of Austin. City planners heeded Mrs. Johnson's call to utilize the gem that Austin has in its lakes. They dedicated several miles of lakefront in downtown Austin for a park and trail network that includes a ten-mile loop around Lady Bird Lake. Countless Austinites and visitors to the city run, walk, and bike that trail every day of the year. And it was on that very trail that I used to run when I was in high school.

The high school I attended, Austin High, sits right off the shores of Lady Bird Lake. Our football coaches used to take advantage of our school's proximity to the trails by making us run several miles a day during our off-season training. As an adult, I have grown to love running. But when I was a student and being forced to run, I hated it. I, along with several other reluctantly running teammates, used to look for any way possible to make the runs more bearable or shorter. It was that search for "shorter" that landed me in hot water with my coach.

Over the years, weary runners have cut little paths through the trees that hug the trails around the lake. These little shortcuts actually don't save a runner much distance—maybe just a few hundred yards. But it makes the run *feel* shorter, and when you don't want to be out there in the first place, every saved yard counts.

Once on a particularly long run, I took one of the shortcuts, along with about ten of my teammates. When I got back to the clubhouse, one of our coaches was outside waiting for us. I really liked this guy. He was nice, fair, but hard-nosed when he needed to be. Most of the players really respected him, and we all wanted to please him.

As we approached the clubhouse, the coach walked right past all my teammates and right up to me. He got in my face and said, "Took a little shortcut, huh?" Of course I was shocked. How did he know? Did someone tell on us? Did he have cameras in the trees, or was it just that omniscience that all coaches seem to possess? That's what it seemed like.

He continued. "Davis, I thought you were a leader. I expected more of you." Then he said five words that almost put me in the fetal position: "I'm so disappointed in you." He might as well have kicked me off the team. He might as well have told me I was going to be shot at sunrise. Nothing—and I mean nothing—hurt worse than being labeled a disappointment.

That was over thirty years ago. I still run those trails in Austin, and I still go by the shortcuts. I've never taken the shortcuts again, not once. Every other runner on the trail may take them, but not me. No way. Not since I heard those words that most of us dread hearing: "I'm so disappointed in you."

What's the Big Deal with Disappointment?

If you go to a dictionary, you'll find that disappointment has to do with unmet expectations. When you hope for or expect one outcome but get another, lesser outcome, the result is disappointment. You have hopes or expectations that the stock market will hit a certain new height; when it doesn't, you're disappointed. You root for your favorite sports team to do well; when they don't play up to your expectations and hopes, you feel let down. You hope and expect to get a certain gift for your birthday; when it doesn't materialize, you feel disappointed.

But no doubt the highest and most painful level of disappointment is with others. You want someone to ask you on a date, you expect a child to do well in math, you want an employer to give you a promotion, or you expect your spouse to be attentive to your needs. And when others—friends, kids, employers, spouses, parents—let us down, the feelings can sometimes be overwhelming.

For many of us, though, the worst part of disappointment is feeling that we have let someone else down. Knowing that we've failed someone we love, care about, or want to impress far surpasses the pain we feel when others have failed us. For me, that one really hurts. Tell me I'm ugly, sentence me to fifty years of hard labor in a prison camp, or even condemn me to an eternity of listening to Barry Manilow songs, but please don't tell me I'm a disappointment. That's just not something I'm secure enough to handle.

Worst of all, I hate feeling like I've disappointed God. Maybe you feel the same. For many of you, the reality of God's ongoing disappointment with you is almost unbearable. He loves you, he died for you, and he saved you. You cherish your relationship with him, and you know what it cost Jesus to make that relationship possible. You feel the least you could do is not break his heart every day. And if you think you've failed him, disappointed him, or made him feel like he can't rely on you or that he made a mistake in trusting you, that thought can be devastating. For some of you, it can be the deal breaker in your walk with God. If you feel like you have really let God down, you may never muster up the courage to turn back to him.

Sound familiar? It does to me. Painfully familiar.

The Lie

You are constantly letting God down. With every new day, he has a fresh and full slate of hopes and dreams for your life, but by the end of each day, he's facing the ugly reality that you've failed to be all that he hoped you would. Once again you haven't lived up to God's expectations.

So goes this lie.

If you think about it, that reasoning makes sense. We're human and sinful. No matter how hard we try and how much we have yielded to sanctification in our lives, we aren't going to be perfect. Even if we perform at a 90 percent level of obedience as a Christian, God would have preferred that we be at 95 percent. Right? Jesus even commanded us to make sure that our righteousness exceeds that of the Pharisees and to be perfect like God is perfect (see Matt. 5:20, 48). I know that on my best days I'm not perfect, and on my worst days I can be downright sinful. Can you relate? How can God *not* be disappointed in us?

But can you see how paralyzing such thinking is to a Christian? After a while, you're bound to succumb to the "what's the point" thinking that comes with a sense that everything you're doing is disappointing God. Because of that, many Christians just quit trying. They believe that at some point in the future, God is going to give up on them, if he hasn't already. And if that's true, they'd prefer to save him the trouble and themselves the pain of experiencing his rejection. So they just give up on their faith, or at least they stop hoping for anything better.

The Truth

God has never been disappointed in you. Not once, ever. The emotion of disappointment is something that he can never feel. Our enemy, the devil, is skilled at painting a picture of God as the brokenhearted—or, worse, angry—deity who has been failed one time too many by us. But that simply isn't true. God has never been and never will be disappointed with you. Let's find out why.

God Knows Everything

Think about it: at the very core of disappointment is a failure to meet expectations. We get disappointed when someone doesn't do what we hope or expect them to do. But if someone knows everything, how can you disappoint him? How can you let down someone who always has the right expectations and understanding in every situation? If we think we can somehow do something that God didn't expect or surprise him in some way, then we seriously underestimate the scope of God's knowledge.

Concerning the limitless nature of God's mind, Isaiah wrote, "Who has understood the mind of the LORD, or instructed him as his counselor? Whom did the LORD consult to enlighten him, and who taught him the right way? Who was it that taught him knowledge or showed him the path of understanding?" (Isa. 40:13–14). In other words, "Who taught God?" Implied answer? No one!

Or what about God's famous question to Job: "Who is this that darkens my counsel with words without knowledge?" (Job 38:2). I'm really glad God asked Job that question and not me. Can you imagine God looking you in the eye and asking, "Uh, excuse me, but I'm just a little curious—why are you trying to outthink me?" Yikes.

Or again, back to Isaiah: "'For my thoughts are not your thoughts, neither are your ways my ways,' declares the LORD. 'As the heavens are higher than the earth, so are my ways higher than your ways and my thoughts than your thoughts'" (Isa. 55:8–9). In other words: "You'll never be able to fully understand my mind. I think on an entirely different level."

God's mind is infinite. He doesn't have any boundaries or limits to his knowledge. Think about all the reason, understanding, and truth that we know today, and all the knowledge and learning that currently lies beyond the reach of our minds—God doesn't just already know all of that, he created it.

God knows our every plan, idea, and intention. He knows the infinite number of futures that could possibly play out based on any number of decisions made by billions of people every day. He knows every possible scenario for every event in history, if any detail, large or small, had gone differently. He knows what would have happened if Moses had not turned aside to look at the burning bush, if David hadn't fought Goliath, and if Judas hadn't accepted the Pharisees' bribe. He knows how history would be different if the South had won the US Civil War, if President Kennedy hadn't been assassinated, and if the officials at NASA had chosen not to launch the shuttle *Challenger* on the frigid morning of January 28, 1986. And he knows how your life would have turned out if you had attended a different college, if you hadn't married the person you did, and if you'd made any number of better or worse decisions each and every day of your life.

How can you let down someone who knows every possible choice you have made and ever will make? With God knowing all that, how are you possibly going to disappoint him? You don't. No way. It's one of those spiritual laws of heaven. It's simply impossible.

God Created You

Besides the fact that God knows everything, God knows everything about *you*. In the same way a computer programmer or a video game creator knows every potential outcome of every keystroke or maneuver, God knows every one of your potential thoughts and actions. At first that may seem a little unsettling, as many of our potential thoughts and actions aren't very appealing. But in reality, it's actually great news. God knows all this about you and still loves you.

That's exactly what the king and poet David was saying when he penned the beautiful Psalm 139. In verses 13–16 he wrote:

> For you created my inmost being;
>   you knit me together in my mother's womb.
> I praise you because I am fearfully and wonderfully
>   made;
>   your works are wonderful,
>   I know that full well.
> My frame was not hidden from you
>   when I was made in the secret place.
> When I was woven together in the depths of the
>   earth,
>   your eyes saw my unformed body.
> All the days ordained for me
>   were written in your book
>   before one of them came to be.

David confessed that nothing about his life escaped God's knowledge, even before he was born. He understood that he was no cosmic accident. David understood that from the moment of his conception, even before he was ever born, God had been forming him. God knew every day of David's life and literally every breath David would take—exactly how many times his heart would beat in his lifetime—before he was ever born.

Now remember, David wasn't perfect. He failed God in some spectacular ways. But was David afraid of him because God knew everything about him? Did he want to try to pull away from God so he wouldn't let him down? No. In fact, David actually wanted more of God. He concluded his great prayer in Psalm 139 by saying, "Search me, O God, and know my heart; test me and know my anxious thoughts. See if there is any offensive way in me, and lead me in the way everlasting" (vv. 23–24). Instead of fleeing God's scrutiny, David welcomed it. It's like he was saying, "Look, God, since I can't hide from you, since you know my thoughts before I think them, I want you to fully know me. Be in the very core, the very essence of my being. If you're going to know me, then know everything about me!"

How are you going to let down a God who not only made you but also knows every single detail of your life? God knows more about you than you do. He's a "you" expert! How are you going to surprise him or somehow do something he didn't expect? You can't. Look in a mirror and know that God is fully aware of who you are and that he has still chosen to be there with you. You couldn't get away from him even if you tried.

God Sent Christ to Die for Your Sins Even Before You Committed Any

The theological concept of forgiveness is much more comprehensive than most of us realize. When God offers forgiveness through Christ, he doesn't make a small or limited proposal. What he offers is a radical, sweeping removal of every sin you have committed or will commit. Several verses in the Bible teach this, but let me highlight just one of them.

In Romans 5, Paul taught that Jesus died for us even while knowing just how sinful we are. He wrote, "But God demonstrates his own love for us in this: While we were still sinners, Christ died for us" (v. 8). Jesus wasn't confused about his mission or the deep need of those he came to save. He understood that his sacrificial death on the cross was for the sake of those who didn't deserve it. He died for sinners—the worst of the worst. Jesus went to the cross fully aware that he was taking the place of murderers, adulterers, liars, thieves, swindlers, rapists, extortionists, kidnappers, child abusers, gossips, drunkards, drug dealers, prostitutes, assassins, terrorists, pornographers, and dictators. Nothing—no sin—escaped his notice.

Name your worst moment as a human. Name that time when you were most selfish, most sinful, most harmful to others. Or perhaps there will be a time in the future when, God forbid, you are at your worst. In both cases, Jesus died for that sin. Past, present, future—Jesus died for it all. And because of that profound reality of his forgiveness, there's no way we can ever do anything that will somehow shock or surprise God.

Exhibit A

Consider Peter. I identify with this outspoken disciple of Jesus on so many levels. He was passionate about his loyalty to Christ and was in some ways the first disciple to really grasp the true nature of Jesus. But he also had a "cuss first, shoot second, and ask questions later" philosophy that often got him in trouble. Peter was a complete mess, but he was also the disciple Jesus nicknamed "the Rock."

Do you think Jesus invited Peter into his inner circle without fully knowing that he was going to misstep, misspeak, and even fail on several occasions? Do you think Jesus was surprised when Peter wanted to call down fire on the Samaritans or when he fell asleep in Jesus' most critical hour of need? No way. Jesus fully vetted Peter. He knew everything about him, and he invited him to be his disciple anyway.

The most obvious example of how Jesus understood Peter's propensity for failure is found in Jesus' prediction of Peter's denials. You probably know the scene. Jesus warned Peter: "Simon, Simon, Satan has asked to sift you as wheat. But I have prayed for you, Simon, that your faith may not fail. And when you have turned back, strengthen your brothers." Peter replied, "Lord, I am ready to go with you to prison and to death." Jesus answered, "Yeah, right!" Actually, that's what I would have said. Here's what Jesus really said: "I tell you, Peter, before the rooster crows today, you will deny three times that you know me" (Luke 22:31–34).

Jesus was under no delusions about Peter's struggles. He warned Peter in advance of his coming colossal failure. He also told Peter that he had already prayed about the entire situation, and he knew Peter would bounce back and become a significant figure in the post-resurrection church. So was he surprised when Peter told the servant girl that he didn't know Jesus? Absolutely not. Jesus saw it coming long before it happened, had prepared for it, and knew exactly how things would play out in the end. And yet—please don't miss this—Jesus called Peter to follow him anyway.

Jesus knew everything about Peter—his strengths and weaknesses, his passion, his lack of good judgment, and his impulsiveness. But knowing all of that didn't keep Jesus from wanting to be with him. The same is true for you.

Come to Me, All You Who Are Weary and Burdened

We need to repent of our bad theology and of believing this lie about our relationship with God. God is way too big and all-knowing for us to ever surprise him or let him down. To assume otherwise diminishes his greatness and power. We need to accept the biblical fact that God knows everything about us and chose to love us anyway.

Then we need to rest in that knowledge. Part of the yoke of Jesus is our being freed from the constant fear that comes from trying never to let down a holy God. The pressure is off, the tension gone. Jesus' death on the cross settled once and for all the debate of whether we can somehow disappoint our heavenly Father. Our standing as believers before God has forever been confirmed by the death and resurrection of Jesus. Nothing can change that. So rest in the peace of knowing that God has already accepted you. Follow Jesus passionately and energetically. Know that when you fall—and you will—your loving heavenly Father will be the first to pick you up. You will never hear him say, "I'm so disappointed in you."

Small Group Discussion Questions

1. Describe a time when you have disappointed someone else. How did you feel?
2. Talk about a time in your life when you feel like you disappointed God. What happened? How did you feel? After that, did things ever get better for you in your relationship with God?
3. In your own words, state why it is impossible for a Christian to disappoint God. What is it about God's character and nature that makes him immune to being disappointed in us?
4. Read Romans 5:8 together, then take turns speaking it to each other as if you were speaking on God's behalf. Say that Jesus died for them with full knowledge of all of their sins—but make it personal. Use their first name; make Romans 5:8 about them.
5. How is the example of Peter and his failure similar to our own failings in our relationship with Christ? How does Peter's example encourage us to keep trying and not quit when we fail God? How did Jesus respond to Peter? How will he respond to us?
6. Who in your life needs to be encouraged with the truth that he or she isn't a disappointment to God? How can you help that person?
7. After studying this chapter, what disappointment or failure do you need to exchange for Jesus' yoke?
8. After reading this chapter, how will you live differently?

4

This Wouldn't Be Happening
If You Were a Better Christian

"If I were a better Christian . . . I mean, if I hadn't had the abortion, then I'd be able to get pregnant."

I can still remember where I was when she said those words. We were at a restaurant. It was a Saturday night. I remember who was there, where we had been, and why we were all still together. I had been a guest teacher in a church service in another city, and several of their leaders and I decided to go out for a traditional post-service dessert and reflection time. It was usually a fun and encouraging time. But on this night, things had gotten heavy.

A close friend of mine and his wife had decided to join us. At some point during the conversation, we started talking about children. My friend's wife, Janey, just sat quietly. She had suffered several terrible miscarriages, and she and her husband longed to have children, but so far their efforts had produced only heartache. Sensing the awkwardness around the table and seeing Janey's obvious discomfort, one of the ladies in the group said, "Janey, we're all so sorry for your losses. I just know God is going to answer your prayers and give you a child." It wasn't said tritely or condescendingly. The woman had spoken what was in her heart and what we all believed.

And then Janey dropped her bombshell. "If I hadn't had the abortion . . ." She was numb, almost unmoved, when she said it. It was like she had no more tears to cry over her loss. Janey looked as if the shame and guilt of her past had sapped all of her ability to hope and pray for anything better. She spoke as if she was letting us in on a secret—something that only she and God knew: *When I had my abortion at age seventeen, I forfeited the right to ever be a mother. Women who abort their babies shouldn't get second chances. My multiple miscarriages are proof of that. I'm reaping what I've sown.*

But beyond that, Janey's childlessness was an indictment of her own faith. You know the thinking: *If I hadn't had the abortion, I wouldn't be having miscarriages. And if I were a better Christian, if I had really loved Jesus, I wouldn't have had the abortion.* Janey seemed resigned to a life of childlessness and to living the rest of her days with the guilt of knowing it was all her fault. If she had been a better Christian, if she hadn't made the poor choices she had, and if she were living a more godly life now, none of this would have happened. God had told her so.

The Lie

If you really loved God, you'd be good. Obviously, you don't love him. Why do you keep falling into the same sin over and over again? Why do you keep failing like you do? You must not be a very serious Christian.

Have you ever heard those lies? I certainly have. I've often wondered if some of the bad events around me happened simply because I wasn't more of a godly man. And when I start thinking that way, I can be sure that shame and guilt aren't far behind.

Speaking of guilt, it goes hand in hand with the "if you were a better Christian" lie. It sounds like this: *This is your fault. You did this. Shame on you. If you were a better Christian, this wouldn't have happened. You are a terrible, terrible person and an embarrassment to God.*

You know it's a lie—either the voice of the devil or the voice of your own shame and guilt—when the message is destructive and condemning. Satan is the father of lies, and his work is to kill, steal, and destroy. When the message you're hearing about your sin, your choices, your heartaches, and your failures tears you down, then you know it's ultimately the devil's work. It's what he does.

Revelation 12:10 identifies Satan as the one who accuses the followers of Christ. Since the devil doesn't tell the truth, he can only accuse with lies. In the early chapters of Job, Satan accused Job before God and questioned Job's motives in living righteously. In Genesis 3, the devil (via the serpent) accused God by saying that he was being unfair to Adam and Eve. In Matthew 4, Satan again accused God of being unfair when he told Jesus he should take matters into his own hands and feed himself.

But we are the devil's favorite targets. He accuses us, telling us how bad we are, what losers we are, and how worthless we are. That's always his message—he tears down; he destroys;

he attacks; he slanders; and he kills hope, peace, and joy. And he wants us to think that we're hearing God. We're not. God doesn't talk like that.

In Psalm 38:4, David prayed, "My guilt has overwhelmed me like a burden too heavy to bear." Sound familiar? Have guilt and shame become close acquaintances? That's how you know you're hearing lies—the end result of what you hear is destructive. When you're being consumed by shame and guilt, you always feel like David did in this verse. It's overwhelming, oppressive, and exhausting.

In Janey's case, her shame and guilt over her abortion were destroying her. They were drowning out her hope for and faith in God's forgiveness. If you feel like your sin is always being thrown back in your face, then you know you're not hearing God. That's just not how he works.

I'm Afraid I Didn't Do Enough

At a recent Pray Big conference, I was approached by a woman after one of the sessions. She appeared to be shy and timid—painfully so. She talked in a quiet voice, almost a whisper.

She told me that she was concerned about her teenage daughter. She was starting to rebel a little and maybe even was questioning her faith. The troubled mom wanted to know how she could pray biblical prayers for her daughter. As we talked, the woman mentioned in passing that her son had gone through a similar rebellion at the same age. Curious, I asked how he had turned out. She told me he had killed himself when he was nineteen. He had never really pulled out of his rebellion. She had prayed and prayed, but he never turned back to God. Obviously, she was terrified that her daughter might be taking her first steps down the same path.

The most tragic part of this conversation was that the woman had fallen prey to the "if you were a better Christian" lie. Somehow her son's suicide was a reflection of her failed faith. She was consumed with guilt. She was convinced that her son's death was her fault. For years Satan had been beating on her with his lies of "You didn't pray enough. You weren't good enough." And she believed him. Not only was this woman gripped by shame, but she was stuck in her pain because of it. God's efforts to heal her of her loss had been thwarted by the death grip of her belief that she had caused her son's suicide. And now that her daughter was starting to show signs of similar behavior, the devil was really wreaking havoc in this woman's life.

Rarely have I seen a Christian so held captive by Satan's lies. That dear woman is a vivid example of just how devastating the "you weren't good enough" lie can be.

The Truth

You can be a committed Christian and still have hard days and seasons. You can be close to Jesus and still end up in a world of trouble. Bad things happen—sometimes it's because of your sin, but often it has nothing to do with you. So if you get a cold, it doesn't mean God is punishing you. If you get a pink slip at your job or a neighbor decides to sue you, it doesn't necessarily mean that you've fallen out of God's good graces. As Christians, we're going to have bad days, but they aren't typically a result of our lack of love for Jesus. The fact is we live in a sinful world. Heartache is bound to come.

Jesus seemed to go out of his way to let his followers know that troubles would find them. But he was also quick to point out that bad things shouldn't be interpreted as a sign that they weren't spiritual enough. Listen to what he said:

> "I have told you these things, so that in me you may have peace. In this world you will have trouble. But take heart! I have overcome the world" (John 16:33).

> "Blessed are those who are persecuted because of righteousness, for theirs is the kingdom of heaven. Blessed are you when people insult you, persecute you and falsely say all kinds of evil against you because of me. Rejoice and be glad, because great is your reward in heaven, for in the same way they persecuted the prophets who were before you" (Matt. 5:10–12).

> "All men will hate you because of me, but he who stands firm to the end will be saved" (Matt. 10:22).

> "Blessed are you when men hate you, when they exclude you and insult you and reject your name as evil, because of the Son of Man" (Luke 6:22).

> "If the world hates you, keep in mind that it hated me first. If you belonged to the world, it would love you as its own. As it is, you do not belong to the world, but I have chosen you out of the world. That is why the world hates you" (John 15:18–19).

Jesus made it clear that troubles were going to come. But don't let Satan lie to you. Those troubles aren't necessarily a sign of your disobedience or your weak faith. Sometimes your troubles will come because of your faith.

Exhibit A

Jesus' disciples gave up everything to follow Christ, and they did so without knowing the end of the story. When they left their respective fishing nets, tax collector's tables, and political causes to follow Jesus, they did so without the benefit of knowing that he would die, rise again, ascend into heaven, and then start the greatest movement in history. Given what little they actually knew about Jesus, their level of faith and commitment to his cause was more than respectable. They had taken great risks to follow him. It's hard to fault them for their lack of faith.

But trouble found them. On one occasion, they had chosen to row with Jesus across the Sea of Galilee. Jesus quickly fell asleep while the disciples managed the trip across the lake. A storm blew in that was so intense the disciples thought they were going to drown.

Think about it: most of these guys were fishermen. They had seen their share of bad storms on the lake and had lived to tell about them. It's safe to assume that they weren't easily intimidated by a sudden lake squall. But this one was different. It was so big and nasty that those seasoned sailors were sure they were going to capsize and drown. Suffice it to say this was the worst storm of their lives. And they were right there with Jesus. They couldn't have been any closer to him or any more submitted to his plans. Yet they were terrified they would die.

That storm had nothing to do with those followers' disobedience or failing faith. They weren't sinning or rebelling when the storm blew in. They were right in the middle of God's will, and trouble still found them.

Exhibit B

Was there a better, more sold-out follower of Jesus in history than the apostle Paul? We'd be hard-pressed to name many. After coming to faith, Paul poured his life into following and promoting Jesus. He received revelations from God that might be matched only by John's vision of Jesus while in exile on the isle of Patmos. Paul gave us insights into doctrine, specifically the doctrine of grace, that aren't found anywhere else in the Bible, and he was the single most prolific contributor to the Bible.

But as committed as he was, Paul knew more than his fair share of troubles. To the believers in Corinth he wrote:

Are they servants of Christ? (I am out of my mind to talk like this.) I am more. I have worked much harder, been in prison more frequently, been flogged more severely, and been exposed to death again and again. Five times I received from the Jews the forty lashes minus one. Three times I was beaten with rods, once I was stoned, three times I was shipwrecked, I spent a night and a day in the open sea, I have been constantly on the move. I have been in danger from rivers, in danger from bandits, in danger from my own countrymen, in danger from Gentiles; in danger in the city, in danger in the country, in danger at sea; and in danger from false brothers. I have labored and toiled and have often gone without sleep; I have known hunger and thirst and have often gone without food; I have been cold and naked. Besides everything else, I face daily the pressure of my concern for all the churches. (2 Cor. 11:23–28)

That's some résumé! If bad things happen because of our lack of faith or because we don't love Jesus enough, then

Paul must have been one of the worst Christians who ever lived. But we know better. If Paul suffered not because he didn't have faith but rather because he possessed a strong and robust faith, why would you assume that you're any different? Sometimes following Jesus and having troubles go hand in hand.

Exhibit C

What about Jesus? He's the holy, sinless Son of God. He was the only person to live a perfect life. He was the only person to get humanity 100 percent right. He was fully committed to following God's will. And yet no human has ever suffered more. Seven hundred years before Jesus' birth, Isaiah said of him, "He was despised and rejected by men, a man of sorrows, and familiar with suffering. Like one from whom men hide their faces he was despised, and we esteemed him not. Surely he took up our infirmities and carried our sorrows, yet we considered him stricken by God, smitten by him, and afflicted" (Isa. 53:3–4).

Did Jesus suffer for his lack of faith? Was he "smitten by God" because he was a bad person or because he didn't love the Father? No. God's path for Christ took him through the valley of the shadow of death. It was Jesus' obedience to God, not his disobedience, that led him there. And like Job's misguided friends who assumed Job was suffering because he had done something wrong, we mistakenly assume that our Christian brothers and sisters, or even we ourselves, are suffering because we've failed God. More often than not, it's just the opposite.

Guilt or God?

There are going to be times when we fail God. Sin, poor choices, and selfish motives will sometimes win the day, and when they do, we will find ourselves having to deal with the consequences of our actions. I have personally had to confess, repent, and heal damaged relationships far more frequently than I care to admit. Even though I passionately love Jesus, sin still haunts me; so do its wages.

But I've learned over the years that when I fail, I must run to—not from—God. You see, we often mistake the voice of guilt for the voice of God. They're not the same, and it's time we learned to discern the difference.

This isn't my best for you. I want more for you than this, much more. You can do better. Aim higher.

That's how the voice of God sounds when he addresses us in our sin. He tells the truth about it, but he does so in a way that motivates us to do better. Behind any conviction or rebuke from God for our sin is his motive of love.

Guilt isn't from God. Commit those four words to memory. If you're feeling overwhelmed by your guilt, then you've yet to hear God. When he speaks about your failings—and he will—he always does so with an upward pull. That's the difference between conviction and guilt.

Everything the Holy Spirit does, including convicting people of sin, glorifies Jesus. The teachings about the Spirit that Jesus gave to the disciples in John 14–16 make it very clear that the Spirit convicts people in a way that draws them to Christ. The "you're a terrible person" message pushes people away from God. It makes them want to run from him and tells them they're a major disappointment to him.

70

That's not the voice of God's Spirit. God's Spirit simply confirms what we usually already know: *You can do better. This isn't God's best for you. Repent, turn back to Jesus, and let's try this again.*

Do you see the difference in the messages? One shames and condemns, the other inspires.

Let's just lay it out plainly so we're clear. Do you want to know how to discern the difference between conviction (which is what God's Spirit does) and guilt (which is not from God)? Consider these comparisons:

Guilt condemns; conviction calls you to something better.

Guilt tears down; conviction builds up.

Guilt kills hope; conviction inspires hope.

Guilt separates you from God; conviction woos you to God.

Guilt is motivated by hate; conviction is motivated by love.

Guilt leaves you feeling worthless; conviction leaves you knowing you can do better.

Guilt seeks to destroy; conviction seeks to restore.

Guilt produces shame and despair; conviction yields holiness and joy.

Can you see the difference? Can you think about the times in your life when you've been held captive by shame and guilt? Don't put up with them. As a Christian, you can expect the Spirit to convict you of your sins; in fact, you probably want him to. But you shouldn't put up with the voices of guilt and shame. They're not from God. Don't tolerate them.

The Rest of the Story

Let's go back to Janey. Shame did not win the day. Guilt did not prevail. In fact, God used her unfortunate choice to have an abortion to actually drive her to his side. Her tragic miscarriages finally forced Janey to turn to God and deal with her own issues of anger, her failure to forgive herself, and her fear that God was punishing her. What she found was grace and healing. God showed her that his grace is more than enough to cover her bad decisions—even the decision to have an abortion.

Not long after our dinner that night, Janey got pregnant again. This time the story ended differently. She gave birth to a beautiful baby girl. Today that baby is a thriving sixteen-year-old. I've met her. She looks just like her mother.

Come to Me, All You Who Are Weary and Burdened

Guilt isn't from God. Miscarriages, bad accidents, tragedies, and so on—when they happen, they're not always our fault. When we are at fault, God calls us to repent and do better. He never shames or tears us down.

Beyond that, don't assume that your troubles always mean that you've failed God. Looking at the Bible, you may find that trouble in fact means you're exactly where you're supposed to be. But no matter the source of the storm, you can be sure that God is in it with you.

It is time for us to set aside the yoke of guilt and shame. That's a heavy burden for us to carry. Jesus died so we wouldn't have to. As Christians, we aren't supposed to live in regret. Yes, we will sin. Yes, we will make poor choices. But they aren't supposed to win the day in our lives. Guilt and shame shouldn't define us. Grace should.

Why not let go of your hurt? Why not leave your shame and guilt at the feet of Jesus? Take up his burden of peace and let him deal with your fears and failings. His shoulders are broad enough to carry all your concerns. Remember, guilt isn't from God. Grace is.

Small Group Discussion Questions

1. In your own words, restate the "if you were a better Christian" lie. Why do you think it's both so common and so powerful?
2. Do you know someone like Janey—someone who is held captive by guilt over a poor choice in the past?
3. Read Revelation 12:10–11. What does it say about the work of Satan in the world and how we overcome him? What three things are critical in our having freedom from Satan's lies?
4. If you were counseling the woman who blamed herself for her son's death, what would you say to her? How could you help free her from her guilt and shame?
5. Read Matthew 5:10–12; 10:22; Luke 6:22; John 15:18–19; and 16:33. How do those verses make you feel? What reasons did Jesus give us for expecting to have trouble in the world?
6. The disciples, the apostle Paul, and Jesus himself all suffered severe hardships in their lives. They were totally committed to and obedient to God, yet they still faced a lot of pain. What does that tell you about your own hardships and suffering? Since you know that bad things still happen to committed followers, how might you counsel Janey to encourage her after her miscarriages?
7. Define *guilt* and then *conviction*. See how many differences you can list between the two. How can you learn to discern the difference between guilt and conviction in your own life?

8. Read John 14:15–18, 25–27; 15:26; 16:5–16; and 1 John 2:1. What can we learn about the work of God's Spirit in our lives from these verses? What characteristics of his voice and his teachings do these Scriptures show us? According to 1 John 2:1, what happens when we sin?

9. What, if any, burden of guilt and shame do you need to release? Where is it from? Are you ready and willing now to let it go and take on Jesus' light yoke?

10. After reading this chapter, how will you live differently?

5

It's Okay Not to Love Certain People

I met Amy on a flight from Edmonton to Denver. She was returning from a weekend of skiing in the Canadian Rockies; I had been leading a Pray Big event in Edmonton. She had the look of an adventurer—early forties, ragged jeans, tattered ski vest, battered backpack, a banged-up ski helmet strapped to her pack, and the raccoon tan of someone who spent a lot of time on the slopes. Yes, I was jealous.

Amy was the outgoing sort, and we immediately struck up a conversation. I had wanted to sleep or just listen to some music on the plane, but Amy's charm and charisma quickly grabbed my attention. There was something about her—not in a romantic or tempting way. It was something else . . . I wasn't sure.

As we talked, I noticed that Amy was quick to throw God and other spiritual terms into her conversation. She talked repeatedly about how blessed she was. She told me that she was single and lived in Boulder, which quickly raised a red flag for me. Boulder, like my hometown of Austin, isn't known for its Christian presence. The Christians who live there and the churches that serve there face an uphill battle with the strong presence of New Age churches and the anything-goes relativism that so many adults embrace. Amy kept mentioning God and his blessings to her, but it was almost like she was trying too hard. It was like she was trying to convince herself, not me, of her spiritual favor.

More of Amy's story spilled out. She had gone to Catholic schools all her life and even attended a Jesuit college. After she graduated, she left home. She hadn't been to church—at least not the Christian kind—since. She'd also had a falling-out with her parents that left their relationship strained at best. She still visited them, but the hurt she felt over the relational rift was obvious. As Amy talked about her folks, a little bit of the light in her eyes faded. There was definite pain there.

Things were starting to fall into place for me. Amy hadn't told me everything, but she had told me enough to help me put the pieces together. I've been a Christ-follower long enough to see the patterns in how people live and move. I've lived in the spiritually confused city of Austin long enough to recognize a broken and hurting person like Amy pretty quickly. In reality, you and I meet people like Amy all the time, they just have different faces.

I asked the obvious question: "Are you gay?"

Amy didn't even hesitate. "Yes."

My question may seem startling to you, but it wasn't really awkward at the time. I knew the answer before I asked the question. Curiously, Amy seemed almost relieved to have her secret out. I think my lack of a response—shock, disgust, condemnation, whatever—surprised her.

The conversation continued. I asked Amy about her childhood, her dad, and her experiences in a strict church-school environment. But Amy didn't place blame on anyone or have any trauma to speak of. As early as she could remember, she had been attracted to women.

Let me clear something up right here: homosexuality is a sin. God didn't create people with gay feelings, and the Bible in no place condones gay practices. But the struggles many homosexuals face are much more complicated than many of us realize, especially for those who have never had a friend, son, daughter, or neighbor who is gay. For many, it's not as easy as "just quitting." Besides that, the Bible doesn't name homosexuality as a sin that's worse than any other. God doesn't hate gays, and a person isn't automatically condemned to hell just because he or she is gay. It's a sin, but it's not *the* sin—even though many churches and Christians preach, teach, and act as if it is.

When Amy told me about her strict religious background, her falling-out with her parents, her lack of church involvement, and her lifestyle, I knew I was talking to someone in a lot of pain. At some point in the conversation she asked what I did, so she knew I was a Christian and a pastor. So far she hadn't shut me out. I think she was surprised that we were having such an easy time talking, given our apparent theological and lifestyle differences.

After a few more minutes of dialogue, I was ready to take a chance with Amy. I said to her, "I want to apologize to you. I want to apologize for how so many in my world—the world I live and serve in—have been so quick to condemn so many in your world." It wasn't very articulate, but I think Amy got my point. She turned away from me and gazed out the airplane window for several long seconds. Then I noticed that her chin was quivering. She was crying. Amy turned back to me and said through her tears, "Thank you. I never thought I'd hear a Christian say that."

The Lie

It's okay to judge. It's okay to condemn. It's okay to write off, avoid, criticize, dislike, and even hate people whose lifestyles repulse you. The more sinful they are, the more it's permissible to bash them.

So goes the insidious lie that many Christians believe gives them permission to attack people they disagree with. If you find their behavior offensive, their politics threatening, or their theology controversial, then you have the right and even the duty to let them and as many others as possible know that you reject their abhorrent thinking and behaviors, and that you will not associate with people who act or think in such ways. This party line teaches that it's a Christian's duty to condemn those who "don't get it" and to openly proclaim his or her resistance to them. Let me offer two public examples:

- A pastor of a large North American church invited then-president Bill Clinton to speak at his church's annual conference on leadership. This was after the president had been impeached and tried for his wrongdoings in the Monica Lewinsky scandal. The pastor received significant public and private resistance to his decision to invite the president. That wasn't the problem. People have the right to oppose decisions their leaders make, and they can do so with solid biblical and logical reasons. But what troubled the pastor was the tenor of so many of the messages he received. Christian pastors wrote and spoke openly of their hatred for the president. Others said they were praying for harm to come to him. And the pastor himself was publicly and repeatedly criticized for having anything to do with a man of such low moral fiber as President Clinton.

- A well-known Christian leader publicly and repeatedly called comedienne Ellen DeGeneres "Ellen Degenerate" because of his opposition to her gay lifestyle.

I could list others. Tragically, the obvious public examples are far outnumbered by the countless other examples of hatred that Christians spew at those they disagree with or feel threatened by. Sadly, Christians somehow have started believing that it's acceptable to be mean. And we do it in Jesus' name.

The Truth

Hate isn't an option for a Christian, at least not when it comes to other people. We can hate sin, the devil, and the evil and injustice in the world, but we don't have the option of hating anyone created in the image of God. The fact that Jesus died for every person, even those whose politics or lifestyles we can't stand, tells us that we must look at others through God's eyes, not our own.

Having said that, it still isn't easy to love those we may adamantly disagree with. So how do we adjust our attitudes and learn to love those who don't appear to be very lovable?

Here is something to keep in mind: *expect lost people to act lost*. This is the most important concept I've learned in the last thirty years of dealing with unbelieving people. They're not Christians, they hold neither my worldview nor my values, and I shouldn't expect them to act like I do. People without Jesus typically live and act in ways that are offensive to people who know Jesus. Our respective worlds are diametrically opposed to each other. And like the mixing of cold air with hot, when you get the two together, there's bound to be chaos.

But getting angry with an unbeliever for how he or she acts is no more effective than getting angry with a sick person for showing symptoms. People without Jesus are sick, but their disease is far more insidious than any physical ailment a doctor will ever treat. When people without Jesus cuss openly or tell filthy jokes, when they lie about their hours at work or lie about their income on their tax returns, when they embrace politics that oppose biblical values, or when they frequent strip clubs, they are doing exactly what their sinful nature is telling them to do. In other words, they're acting naturally. You can't expect people with a nature under the control of sin to act like they're under the control of God's Spirit. They're not, and hating them for their spiritual disorder isn't just unfruitful, it's unbiblical.

Exhibit A

When I was in school, Susie and I lived in a small rental house in a lovely part of Fort Worth, Texas. We lived at the end of a street, and our house's property was adjacent to a beautiful park. We loved the area and felt blessed to live there. Next door was a duplex, and the couple in the unit closest to us was delightful. They were Christians and shared our desire for a quiet, peaceful existence and keeping our children safe. We really enjoyed having them as neighbors.

Then they moved away and Kevin moved in. Kevin was the complete opposite of our first neighbors. He was single; he didn't keep up his yard; he consistently held wild, late-night parties; and I seriously believe he was dealing drugs out of his house.

One night Susie and I and both of our children were awakened by a loud crash against our house. When I went outside to investigate, I found a broken beer bottle lying in our yard. It had been thrown against the wall right next to our daughter's bedroom by one of Kevin's friends. Needless to say, I was furious. It was one thing for Kevin to party in his own yard, but quite another for his rude behavior to spill over into mine.

Not long after, Kevin got a roommate whose name was Tonya. She was an attractive young lady who was taking a semester off from school and working for her dad. She and Kevin were living lives completely opposite to Susie and me. They really bugged us. They were sleeping together outside of marriage, doing and dealing drugs, and, in my humble opinion, ruining our neighborhood. I really didn't like them or care for their lifestyle.

I've neglected to mention that while I was living next door to Kevin and Tonya, I was a pastor and a doctoral student at one of the largest theological institutions in the world. If there was anyone on earth who should have understood why my neighbors were acting as they did, it was me. If anyone should have been able to muster up some compassion for these two obviously lost people, it was me. And if anyone should have known that lost people act lost, that we are all the same before God, and that I was in need of grace as much as my drug-dealing neighbors, well, it was me. I was being trained on a postgraduate level to lead churches to reach people like Kevin and Tonya. God had dropped two card-carrying lost people right next door to me, two people I could love in Jesus' name, and I was too arrogant to see it.

The Holy Spirit, however, was working on me. I got convicted about my attitude toward my neighbors and began praying for a chance to witness to them. And then Tonya's car broke down in front of my house. It sat there, right in front of my porch, for nearly two weeks. And every day it sat there, I got angrier and angrier. It was like salt on the already open wound of my dislike and disgust for my neighbors. I never made the connection between my prayer for a chance to witness to them and the opportunity the Spirit had given me to serve them by helping Tonya with her car.

Finally, I walked over one day and knocked on their door. Tonya came to the door, looking high. I asked her to move her car. She said she was waiting for her dad to come work on it and that she would move it when she could.

That's it. That's the extent of my evangelistic efforts with my lost neighbors. Tonya knew me as the irritated neighbor who wanted her to move her clunker away from the front of his house. She didn't know me as the follower of Jesus who had been strategically placed next door to her to help her see the love of the Savior who had died for her.

After my conversation with Tonya, things got quiet next door. We didn't see or hear from Kevin or Tonya for several weeks. Her car had been moved, and the house was quiet and still. It was as if God had answered our prayers. We were happy.

Several weeks later, I was driving home from church. It happened to be Easter, and I was wearing my Sunday best and still glowing from the awesome Easter services I had just participated in. It was springtime in Fort Worth, so the flowers were out and church attendance was up. Things couldn't have been any better.

As I turned onto my street, I saw Kevin's car in his and Tonya's driveway. Before I had time to react, I saw Kevin trying to get out of his car. I say "trying" because his arm was in a huge cast. He had a full cast from his wrist up to his shoulder. It wasn't in a sling; rather, it was supported by a metal brace that protruded from his hip, which kept his arm extended from his body at a right angle. It was so big and awkward that he was having trouble getting out of his small car.

I stopped in front of my house and immediately walked up to Kevin. This time my concern for him was real. He had obviously been seriously injured.

I greeted him. "Kevin, what happened? Are you okay?"

He answered, "You didn't hear? Tonya's dead."

He continued talking. He said something about a terrible car crash in Dallas . . . seven people in the car . . . he was driving . . . Tonya didn't make it.

I really didn't hear much of what he said. It was as if I had been punched in the stomach. I immediately felt sick and wanted to throw up. I mumbled something to Kevin about how sorry I was and how I was there if he needed me. I've probably never spoken emptier or more meaningless words in my life. God had given me the perfect opportunity to love two lost people. Instead, I had treated them as my enemies. They were acting exactly as their respective sin natures were telling them to. I was just too impatient and holier-than-thou to see what was really going on.

I have no idea how things might have been different if I had chosen to love Tonya and Kevin. I'll never know. But here's what I do know—I have no reason to believe that Tonya was a Christian, and now she's dead. I have to live with that the rest of my life.

A Much Better Example

Jesus once met a demon-possessed man who was literally out of control. He was a threat to others and to himself. The biblical writer Mark offered this synopsis of the story:

> They went across the lake to the region of the Gerasenes. When Jesus got out of the boat, a man with an evil spirit came from the tombs to meet him. This man lived in the tombs, and no one could bind him any more, not even with a chain. For he had often been chained hand and foot, but he tore the chains apart and broke the irons on his feet. No one was strong enough to subdue him. Night and day among the tombs and in the hills he would cry out and cut himself with stones. (Mark 5:1–5)

For me, that demon-possessed man represents people like Kevin and Tonya. They're under the influence of something dark and insidious, something they probably don't see or understand in themselves. They're harmful to others and to themselves. They also frighten and threaten us. My tendency is to judge, resist, or just ignore such people. But as a follower of Jesus, I don't have those options. When I learn to see people as God sees them, when I learn to see them with eyes of compassion, and when I realize that Jesus is greater than any forces of darkness that may control them, then my heart will change and I will be compassionate toward them.

Jesus set a great example for us in how he dealt with this demon-possessed man. Instead of running from him or being disgusted by his condition, Jesus walked right into his world. He met the man where he was, loved him as he was, and then set him free from all that bound him. Mark's description of the man after he met Jesus says it all: "When they came to Jesus, they saw the man who had been possessed by the legion of demons, sitting there, dressed and in his right mind" (Mark 5:15).

That's what Jesus wants to do for every Kevin and Tonya in our lives. If we will see past their sin and recognize the impoverished condition of their souls, then God can use us to help set them free.

Loving Kevin and Tonya

Overcoming our natural prejudice against unbelievers may not come naturally. Unless you have a gift of evangelism or high degrees of compassion, you may have to work at loving those whose lifestyles offend you. Here are some suggestions for changing how you view the unbelieving:

Study the Bible. Scripture gives us clear and graphic descriptions of the condition of those without Christ. It also tells us quite emphatically how God feels about them. As you read and study the Bible, ask God to help you to see unbelievers from a biblical standpoint. Ask him to give you his heart of compassion for them.

Pray for them. Fill your prayer journal with the names of unbelievers. Pray for the people in the world whom you find most offensive. I have personally found this practice to be effective. I pray regularly for some of the world's best-known and most outspoken atheists. I also pray for political leaders and other public figures who have made no secret of their disdain for Christ and his followers. I pray that God would remove their public platforms, humble them, and then help them to see and receive the love of Christ.

Serve them. Recently a woman asked me how she could love her enemies. In her case, it was Muslims. She despised them. She knew her feelings were wrong, but she was powerless and rather unmotivated to change. Besides telling her to study the Scriptures and to pray, I told her to serve them. I encouraged her to find a group of Muslims who were in need of some type of care and to meet their needs.

Serving your enemies is the fastest way to learn to love them. It will help you to see them through the eyes of compassion, and it will humble you. Serving is also a great platform from which you can share Jesus' love with a seeking person.

Come to Me, All You Who Are Weary and Burdened

It doesn't suit us as Christians to be judgmental and hateful. It's completely inconsistent with the Spirit of Christ in us. Jesus came to seek and to save the lost. When he inhabited you at the moment of your salvation, he turned you into a vessel of seeking and saving others. Don't resist his work in you by resisting those around you whom he is looking for.

Carrying the yoke of a judgmental, critical, and fearful spirit is exhausting. Carrying the yoke of hate is equally burdensome. But love weighs very little. It's a pleasant and refreshing yoke to carry.

Are you feeling overwhelmed by always trying to oppose certain types of people? Are you weary from keeping at arm's length those whose lives, politics, beliefs, and behaviors are threatening to yours? Is your hate eating you up?

Let it go. Take on Jesus' yoke of love. "Therefore, as God's chosen people, holy and dearly loved, clothe yourselves with compassion, kindness, humility, gentleness and patience. Bear with each other and forgive whatever grievances you may have against one another. Forgive as the Lord forgave you. And over all these virtues put on love, which binds them all together in perfect unity" (Col. 3:12–14).

You'll find it a much more enjoyable way to live.

Small Group Discussion Questions

1. What did you think of the opening story about Amy? Have you ever felt judged or rejected by another Christian?

2. Why do we sometimes think it is permissible to judge or even hate others? Why do others' lifestyles or beliefs often threaten us?

3. Restate the "lost people act lost" principle in your own words. Why is it imperative for us to remember that when we are dealing with unbelieving people?

4. Name some people you know today who are acting lost. How should you respond to them?

5. Summarize the story of Kevin and Tonya. How did it make you feel?

6. Are there any Kevins and Tonyas in your life? Who has God placed in your world so you can help them to see Jesus?

7. How can you change your heart toward unbelievers?

8. After reading this chapter, how will you live differently?

6

Everyone Should Believe and Act like You Do

Years ago, when I was still in school and leading a small church in Fort Worth, I started a prayer ministry in our church. It was called the Swollen Knees Prayer Ministry. A buddy of mine had visited our church and preached about how prayer warriors should have swollen knees. I thought the phrase was cool, so I stole it for our new ministry.

The Swollen Knees Prayer Ministry—pretty warm and fuzzy, huh? The goal of the ministry was to cover all 168 hours of the week in prayer, with each participant taking at least one hour. Given that we barely had 168 adults in the church, that was a pretty ambitious goal. Being the godly, sacrificial pastor that I was (and as a legalist, believing that if prayer didn't hurt, it didn't count), I took Saturday mornings from 2:00 to 3:00 a.m. I would set my alarm for 1:50 a.m., take the relay call from the 1:00 to 2:00 person, and then try to pray from 2:00 to 3:00. We had a prayer script that we could follow, and I would sleepily work my way through that. Then I'd call the 3:00 to 4:00 person and fall back into bed. It was a really tough hour to pray. But because it was so hard, I knew it had to be effective. I also knew that I was a very spiritual person because I prayed from 2:00 to 3:00 a.m.

My wife, Susie, wasn't quite so spiritual. She took the 8:00 to 9:00 p.m. Saturday night shift. I mean, what gives? Where's the sacrifice? Where's the commitment? Anyone can pray at 8:00 in the evening. And to make matters worse, she had fun doing it.

I remember walking into our back room one Saturday night during Susie's allotted prayer time. She was riding our Schwinn exercise bike with her headphones on. She was singing and waving her hands in the air and smiling. (Smiling? Are you serious? You can't smile during prayer.) She had her prayer script nearby, but it was obvious she wasn't using it.

I couldn't believe it. My own wife was cheating at prayer. I pointed a mean, accusatory finger at Susie and yelled, "That doesn't count!" We're still paying that counseling bill.

Graduate-Level Legalism

What is it about Christians that makes us want to legislate how others live out their faith? Why are we so quickly threatened by how others worship, pray, serve, behave, and even believe on certain points? It's obvious from the New Testament that there wasn't a uniformity of practice and behavior among the early Christians, and Paul even addressed that in some of his letters. But the finger pointing and accusing goes on, and the winds of grace continue to be stifled.

Why is that? For a people who boast a faith that provides freedom and liberty from rule keeping, we are quick to impose rules and regulations on others. Have you ever heard or said any of these?

I don't lift my hands in worship, so you shouldn't either.

We serve the poor and give away lots of money, so you should too.

I don't let my kids see R-rated movies; you're a bad Christian if you do.

We don't dance; all Christians who do are sinning.

You shouldn't listen to secular music, just Christian.

You shouldn't listen to Christian music with a certain beat; it's from Satan.

If you don't homeschool, you're not godly.

We don't drink alcohol. It's wrong for all Christians.

Christians who smoke shouldn't be allowed in the church.

We don't use credit cards. If you do, you're not a good steward.

Your church's ten-million-dollar building program is totally selfish and grandiose. That money should be given to missions.

You're not a stay-at-home mom? How can you call yourself a Christian mother?

Christian Democrat is an oxymoron.

If you weren't immersed, then your baptism didn't count.

If you don't read this translation of the Bible, you're not a thinking Christian.

We don't ordain women to ministry, and we don't fellowship with churches that do.

If you're not a five-point Calvinist, you're not a very so-
phisticated Christian.

If you believe in the gift of tongues, you're a liberal.

If you believe in any form of evolution, you're probably
not a Christian.

Christians who don't believe in the young-earth theory of
creation are worshiping the god of science.

Christian musicians who cross over and do rock, pop, or
country have sold out to consumerism and abandoned
their faith.

Play That Funky Music

My wife, Susie, used to work for a family-friendly radio station here in Austin. It was a commercial station owned by a
large for-profit company that had dozens of stations around
the country. It played a lot of Christian hits, but it also played
some popular and clean songs by non-Christian artists. It
was the kind of music I listen to in my car and on my iPhone
(only I listen to a lot more Doobie Brothers and Toto than
the station played).

It was really disheartening to hear all the mean-spirited
and judgmental criticism that Susie and her cohosts received
from Christians who didn't like their music mix. Because they
played both Christian and non-Christian music, people accused them of all sorts of spiritual failings. The worst was the
woman who called in and told them that she was concerned
they had all lost their salvation.

Seriously? My wife is no longer a Christian because she likes to listen to Phillips, Craig & Dean *and* Coldplay? My daughters love Taylor Swift. Does that mean that they're in spiritual peril as well?

Can you see how judgmental and hypocritical such thinking is? How did we as Christians ever get in the business of trying to legislate each other's behavior? And perhaps more importantly, why do we do it?

The Lie

If it's wrong for you, then it has to be wrong for everyone else. If God requires you to do it, then every other Christian has to do it too. If we're not all completely uniform in our Christian beliefs and practices, then someone is out of line. If others aren't acting, worshiping, and believing exactly as you do, then they're not good Christians. Maybe they're not Christians at all.

That's the lie many Christians believe. Jesus never set up a standard by which all Christians were to be judged. Oh wait, I'm wrong on that. He actually did give us a standard, sort of a Christian universal standard of behavior. It's love. Unfortunately, love has given way to judging, and grace has been replaced by score keeping. Sadly, many churches have become breeding grounds for legalism.

I'm Okay, You're Not

What is legalism? It is the practice of establishing standards for spiritual performance, in addition to or instead of God's, and expecting that you and others will adhere to them. It's a works-oriented spirituality based on what a person does, not on who he or she is becoming in Christ. It puts the responsibility for gauging someone's spiritual progress or maturity in the hands of people, not God.

A legalist is someone who majors in rule keeping. Their relationship with God is reduced to a series of rules and regulations that must be strictly enforced and applied to all believers. Rule keeping is convenient because it's measurable and tangible. People who love lists and step processes often fall prey to the snare of legalism because it looks so pragmatic on the surface. The legalist's mantra is "Just do A, and B will happen."

But the reality is that legalism sucks the life right out of faith. There is no love required in rule keeping, and it breeds the mind-set that God somehow owes us a break because we're trying so hard and because we're so much better than many other Christians. Here are a few common characteristics of legalists:

They can't celebrate other Christians' successes. Legalists can't stand to see another believer prospering. They can't believe that anyone could be trying harder than they are, so no one deserves God's favor more than they do. Legalists are typically envious of and even hateful toward other believers.

They feel the need to defend themselves. Good legalists don't understand grace, so they can't afford to have a bad day. When they do fail, they're not able to really own up to it and confess it. Legalists have to make excuses and defend themselves; otherwise they'd have to admit that their best efforts aren't working.

They feel entitled. Legalists believe that God owes them favor and blessing. Their rule keeping and hard work have surely merited some special treatment from God.

They want what God can do for them more than they want to be with him. True legalists don't understand that Christianity is deeply rooted in love. Theirs is not a father/son or father/daughter relationship. It's more of an employer/employee or commander/soldier relationship. Legalists view God as someone to be appeased so they can get what they need or want from him. Their goal is God's presents, not God's presence.

They can't extend grace to others. Those who live by rule keeping judge others by the same standard. Legalists can't afford to extend grace to someone who fails. That violates the whole rule-keeping mind-set. If someone fails, it's simply because they weren't trying hard enough. They deserve not grace but consequences. Because legalists live by the "I can" mind-set, they aren't quick to extend grace to those who can't.

They typically struggle with secret sin. The spiritual bankruptcy of the rule-keeping life will inevitably lead to a great deal of emotional and spiritual pain. Legalists won't be able to live up to their own standards and will have to deal with the obvious duplicity of what they say on one hand and do on the other. Such ongoing shame and inner conflict will typically lead to some type of secret sin such as binge eating, alcoholism or workaholism, prescription drug abuse, or a pornography habit, as the struggling legalists will seek to medicate the pain that is flowing out of their failing and flawed religious system.

Do any of those tendencies sound familiar? Do you think that maybe you have a little legalist in you? Most of us do. But there is great news for all of us weary rule keepers out there, especially if we're worn out from carrying the yoke of trying to regulate everyone else's behavior.

The Truth

Rather than giving you my own words here, let's let the Bible speak for itself:

> "It is for freedom that Christ has set us free. Stand firm, then, and do not let yourselves be burdened again by a yoke of slavery" (Gal. 5:1).

> "Do not judge, or you too will be judged. For in the same way you judge others, you will be judged, and with the measure you use, it will be measured to you" (Matt. 7:1–2).

> "You, therefore, have no excuse, you who pass judgment on someone else, for at whatever point you judge the other, you are condemning yourself, because you who pass judgment do the same things" (Rom. 2:1).

> "You, then, why do you judge your brother? Or why do you look down on your brother? For we will all stand before God's judgment seat" (Rom. 14:10).

> "God works in different ways, but it is the same God who does the work in all of us" (1 Cor. 12:6 NLT).

> "Why do you look at the speck of sawdust in your brother's eye and pay no attention to the plank in your own eye? How can you say to your brother, 'Let me take the speck out of your eye,' when all the time there is a plank in

your own eye? You hypocrite, first take the plank out of your own eye, and then you will see clearly to remove the speck from your brother's eye" (Matt. 7:3–5).

"Therefore, there is now no condemnation for those who are in Christ Jesus" (Rom. 8:1).

The great news of the Christian gospel is that God doesn't condemn his children for either their past or their present behaviors. And since God doesn't condemn us, we certainly can't justify condemning each other. Christian legalism is a slap in the face to the grace that Jesus died to give us. It undermines the work of the cross and reduces the Christian message to nothing more than another "it's all up to you" religious program.

Exhibit A

The temptation to impose rules on other Christians isn't a new one. The early church leaders dealt with it repeatedly. Acts 15 records the discussion at a conference the church leaders held in Jerusalem to decide whether or not Gentile men who had come to faith in Christ needed to be circumcised. In other words, did they have to become Jews before they could become Christians? And if they did, would they be required to keep other parts of the Mosaic law as well—like not eating certain foods and honoring the Sabbath? Fortunately, the Spirit prevailed at the Jerusalem Council, and the leaders decided not to require people to keep the Mosaic law as part of being a Christian.

In the book of Galatians, Paul talked about his own confrontation with this early and insidious form of Christian legalism. He wrote that some of the most notable leaders in the early church movement, including Barnabas and Peter, had fallen prey to the temptation to create hoops for the new Gentile believers to jump through. Paul was both disgusted and infuriated by the foolishness and hypocrisy of these leaders. They knew firsthand that the grace of Jesus alone was required to make a person right with God.

Paul finally reached his breaking point. In the setting of a public meal with several church leaders present, Paul called Peter out on his hypocrisy: "You are a Jew, yet you live like a Gentile and not like a Jew. How is it, then, that you force Gentiles to follow Jewish customs?" (Gal. 2:14). In other words, "Hey, Peter, you're a Jew and yet you're not following the law. How dare you require these God-fearing Gentiles to keep rules that you're not even keeping!"

How would you have liked to be a fly on the wall during that conversation? Talk about intense! But Paul was right to rebuke Peter, and we need to hear the same rebuke today. The Christian message has never been about rule keeping. God works in different people in different seasons and in different ways. For some, he leads them to fast regularly; others feel no such leading. Some believers are convicted that drinking is wrong; others believe that wine or beer taken in moderation is fine. One group of Christians enjoys energetic, loud worship; others seek quiet contemplation. Both are right and pleasing in God's eyes, and neither group should judge the other.

The point is that God gives us grace as we live out our sanctification. We need to give it to each other as well. "Accept him whose faith is weak, without passing judgment on disputable matters. One man's faith allows him to eat everything, but another man, whose faith is weak, eats only vegetables. The man who eats everything must not look down on him who does not, and the man who does not eat everything must not condemn the man who does, for God has accepted him" (Rom. 14:1–3).

I've Got the Spirit, Yes, I Do. I've Got the Spirit, How 'Bout You?

Over the past few years, I've become close friends with a Christian musician and pastor who lives here in Austin. Randy Phillips sings with the award-winning group Phillips, Craig & Dean and is the senior pastor of PromiseLand West Church. I don't even remember how Randy and I met, but when we did, we became instant friends. Susie and I consider Randy and his wife, Denise, to be two of our closest friends.

Randy grew up in a charismatic church. Speaking in tongues; prayer languages; and exuberant, passionate worship events were a normal part of his experience. I grew up Southern Baptist, and even though I've really loosened up over the years, my experiences and comfort zones are nowhere near Randy's.

Randy and I know we probably have theological differences, although we've never really talked about them. I am very open to the present reality of all the gifts of the Spirit listed in the Bible, and many Christians whom I deeply love and admire have prayer languages. On the other hand, I have a pretty firm belief about the baptism of the Holy Spirit and when it comes to a believer. I don't know for sure, but I suspect that Randy believes otherwise.

Rather than this being a point of contention for us, our differences have made us closer. Randy and I are good for each other. We remind each other that not every Christian believes and worships in exactly the same ways. We respect and love each other, even though we know we don't agree.

We also tease each other incessantly. Randy is fond of saying to me, "You know, Davis, if you ever get the Holy Spirit, you'll be a great Christian." I always respond by saying, "Randy, if you ever get saved, you'll be a great Christian too."

I'm Okay, You're Okay

How can we learn to extend grace to others? How can we grow comfortable with other Christians who may feel differently about theology, worship styles, or even certain moral issues? Here are a few suggestions:

Give other Christians permission to be different from you. You're not the only Christ-follower in the world, and neither are you the most committed. Your way of loving Jesus is neither the only way nor the best. If you don't know that, your Christian world is way too small. Get comfortable with the wonderful biblical reality that God has followers all over the world who are different from you.

Keep your mouth shut and pray. Before you spout off to a person about her behavior—or, worse, before you spout off to someone *else* about that person's behavior—pray for her. If you have a problem with another believer's actions or beliefs, take it up with God. Don't talk about it to others.

Remember that God is still working on others, and on you. Philippians 1:6 reminds us that salvation is a process. No one is ever completely saved and sanctified until they get to heaven. So give them some room to iron out their pre-Christ wrinkles. They're not perfect, and neither are you.

Practice the discipline of confession. Confession is good for the soul. It's also really good for a legalist. Being brutally honest about your own sin gets you in the habit of not trying to spot that speck in your brother's eye while you're tripping over the telephone pole that's protruding from yours. Getting real about yourself will keep you from getting on another's case.

Keep your mouth shut and pray. Did I mention not to slander or gossip about other Christians? Don't talk about them; pray for them.

Know the difference between the gospel according to the New Testament and the gospel according to you. It's good that you have strong convictions about certain things, and you need to live your life accordingly. But not all Bible-believing Christians agree on everything, especially when it comes to what's right and wrong. Classic gray matters—such as drinking, dancing, music styles, worship styles, types of dress and makeup for women, what's permissible entertainment and what isn't, homeschool versus private school versus public school, and even political persuasions—may not be as clear-cut as you think they are or as you may want them to be. Be biblically literate enough to know where the Bible draws clear lines around certain beliefs, practices, and behaviors, and where it doesn't. God may indeed convict you that a certain behavior is wrong for you. But it may not be an open-and-shut biblical case for others. So don't judge those who believe differently.

Keep your mouth shut and pray! Did I say that already?

Come to Me, All You Who Are Weary and Burdened

Maybe it's time for you to get off your high horse. Maybe it's time for you to stop trying to control everyone else's behavior. That's a heavy burden indeed. God really is big enough and strong enough to manage all the worship styles, behavioral differences, and theological nuances that crop up in his church. He doesn't need your help. Really.

I know from firsthand experience just how exhausting a legalistic lifestyle can be. Grace is much more refreshing. So give yourself and others a break. Let God be in charge. The kingdom isn't going to cave in if other believers in your world act a little differently than you do. Take joy in the fact that your name (and theirs) is written in the Lamb's Book of Life. Release your fears, concerns, and jealousies to Jesus. Pray for God's kingdom to come and his will to be done in the lives of those you're worried about. And then pray the same for your own life.

Today, take on Jesus' yoke of grace. It's a much better burden.

Small Group Discussion Questions

1. What is legalism? Try to come up with a group definition for it.
2. Why do we resort to being legalistic? What's appealing about a rules-based system?
3. Review the list of legalistic statements offered in the "Graduate-Level Legalism" section. Have you ever heard or said any of those? Can you add a few statements not listed there?
4. There are several characteristics of legalists in the "I'm Okay, You're Not" section. Talk for a few minutes about each of them. Do any describe you? Which characteristic do you think you've seen demonstrated the most in your Christian community?
5. Read the verses offered in "The Truth" section. As a group, summarize the main point of each of them. Which verse is most meaningful to you personally? Why?
6. Why did the author say that his relationship with Randy is good for them both? How much opportunity do you have to serve, worship, or just spend time with Christians who may express their faith differently from you? What could you do to broaden your exposure to other Christians? Why would that be important for you?
7. Talk about the steps for learning to extend grace to others in the "I'm Okay, You're Okay" section. Which seems most important to you personally? Why?
8. Would you say that you've been carrying the yoke of judgmentalism or legalism? Why or why not?
9. After reading this chapter, how will you live differently?

7

It's All Up to You

My mother is a walking, talking medical miracle. On March 6, 1997, she got septicemia from a common bladder infection. In a twenty-four-hour period, every major organ in her body shut down, including her heart. She also had a mild stroke. By the time I was able to get to the hospital, she was in a coma and on life support. When I asked the ICU doctor what he was most concerned about for my mother, he replied, "Pick an organ." My mom was sixty-five at the time, and as of the time of this writing, she's still going strong.

Through countless prayers, great medical care, and my mom's own tenacity, she survived that early crisis period. All of her organs eventually started working again except for her kidneys. They took the next seven years off, five of which my mom spent on dialysis. She eventually stopped dialysis and went into hospice care expecting to die from kidney failure, but she never did. Hospice actually fired her for not cooperating. She has an "I survived hospice" T-shirt, but that's another story.

One of the side effects of my mom's stroke was a temporary loss of her hearing. For about a year she used hearing aids, but even with the aids, her hearing was sketchy at best.

One night our entire family went out for dinner to celebrate my mom's persistence and improving health. The restaurant was loud, which made it almost impossible for my mom to hear any of the conversation.

At one point in the dinner, my dad leaned over and asked her how she was doing.

She responded, "What?"

"How are you doing?" he asked again.

"What? I can't hear you," she answered.

Again from Dad, but much louder: "How are you doing?"

And again from Mom, this time with her hand cupped to her ear and yelling nearly as loud: "I still can't hear you."

My dad, not ever being known for his patience and clearly at the end of his rope for the evening, simply yelled back, "Try harder!" The good news is my mom didn't hear him.

Blessed Are Those Who Try Really Hard

It is impossible for a person to make himself or herself godlier by trying really hard. That's no more effective than telling a hearing-impaired person to try harder to hear.

Take Clyde, for example. Clyde is a fifty-two-year-old CPA with a wife and three kids, all grown. He's been a Christian since he was nine. He's a deacon in his church and once did a four-year run as his church's treasurer. He has taught Sunday school and even participated in Monday night church visitation a few times. Clyde reads his Bible, prays regularly, and rarely misses church. He doesn't drink except for the occasional wedding and after the end of a really hard tax season. Clyde's friends are typically churchgoers, although few know Clyde really well. Most of Clyde's clients know he's a religious man.

On the surface, Clyde looks like a pretty good Christian. He appears to be doing everything right. But there is one major problem with Clyde's faith, one chink in his spiritual armor—it's fruit, or the lack thereof. The whole love, joy, peace, patience list that Paul offered as evidence of the Spirit's presence in our lives (see Gal. 5:22–23) never seems to be on Clyde's radar. It's like he missed that memo.

Even with all of Clyde's spiritual and church activities, he can be downright mean. He's short-tempered with his wife and yells at other drivers in traffic. He frequently snaps at his co-workers and has gone through some very bumpy seasons with his children. He's even been in counseling with his oldest. To his credit, Clyde has worked really hard on being more patient, and sometimes he can have pretty good days. But when he's tired, stressed, or not feeling well, his patience goes right out the window. And when that happens, look out. Clyde can be extremely hotheaded and rude when he's at the end of his rope.

Clyde has prayed about his anger issues and lack of patience, but they never really seem to get better. As a result, he's kind of given up. Heaven knows that he has tried really, really hard.

The Lie

It's all up to you.

That's how this lie sounds in its simplest form. It says you may be saved by grace, but you are sanctified (made holy) by what you do. It's on you to stop being so angry, to overcome lust, to start being more loving, and to not want to sin anymore. Jesus gets you to heaven, but you have to do the rest.

Bewitched

In the third chapter of Galatians, the apostle Paul addressed this topic with the Christians in Galatia. They had somehow fallen into the thinking that it was up to them to make themselves right before God. So Paul addressed the issue head-on:

> Oh, foolish Galatians! Who has cast an evil spell on you? For the meaning of Jesus Christ's death was made as clear to you as if you had seen a picture of his death on the cross. Let me ask you this one question: Did you receive the Holy Spirit by obeying the law of Moses? Of course not! You received the Spirit because you believed the message you heard about Christ. How foolish can you be? After starting your Christian lives in the Spirit, why are you now trying to become perfect by your own human effort? Have you experienced so much for nothing? Surely it was not in vain, was it? I ask you again, does God give you the Holy Spirit and work miracles among you because you obey the law? Of course not! It is because you believe the message you heard about Christ. (Gal. 3:1–5 NLT)

That is quite a stinging rebuke from Paul. But his point clearly wasn't lost on the Galatians, and it shouldn't be lost on us. God, through Paul's words, wants us to understand the nature of the Christian walk. It's a life of faith. It's a spiritual process from beginning to end. If the work of God's Spirit is required to get the process started, why would we assume that we can somehow take over the process halfway through? Why, after getting started with the power of God, would we try to revert to living in our own strength?

Suppose you catch an airplane flying from New York to LA. Once you realize the plane is at its cruising altitude of 32,000 feet, would you walk to the cabin door, thank the pilots for their help, and then step outside as if you were going to handle things from there? Obviously not. So why would you assume that you're expected to take over a process that is miraculous from start to finish?

The redemptive work of God in a sinner is a complete miracle. Only God can regenerate a lost soul, and only he can make that soul holy. Believing that I can somehow bring about spiritual change in my life through my hard work insults and cheapens the work of God's Spirit in me. I can't help God; only he can help me.

A Wolf in Sheep's Clothing

I hate to confess this, but for many years I was the founder, president, and CEO of the Try Harder Club in my Christian circles. I could blame my flawed thinking on many things, but it wasn't anyone's fault but my own. Somewhere along the way I began to believe that it was all up to me to live a God-honoring life. The only way to know for sure that I was pleasing God was to keep score. If I read the Bible, prayed, tithed, witnessed, and did any number of other spiritual works, I would surely make God happy.

To make matters worse, I was a pastor. I actually had a platform from which I could share my try-harder doctrine: God wasn't about grace, God was about doing. The more you did for God, the better off you were. And if you weren't doing, you needed to seriously question your Christian commitment.

I spent the better part of a decade calling poor, exhausted sinners to come and work their hearts out for God. I closely resembled the Pharisees Jesus rebuked in Matthew 23:15: "Woe to you, teachers of the law and Pharisees, you hypocrites! You travel over land and sea to win a single convert, and when he becomes one, you make him twice as much a son of hell as you are." I wasn't very good at winning people to Christ, but I was great at winning them to Christianity.

I was far from righteous. The secret sins quickly won the day in my heart. I had a significant amount of pain and dysfunction from my own bad choices growing up, and now I was compounding things by preaching a system that I myself wasn't even keeping. I was the ultimate hypocrite. I looked really committed, I was quick to condemn those who failed, I told people to keep the rules—and yet I was an absolute mess.

My spiritual house of cards collapsed in a heap in the summer of 1996. The pain and guilt of not practicing what I was preaching, the shame of secret sin, and the spiritual bankruptcy that always comes with the try-harder mind-set all caught up with me. I had a complete spiritual, emotional, and physical breakdown. I walked out of the church I was pastoring, unsure if I would ever return, unsure if I was even a Christian.

If trying hard was enough to make you holy, then I should have been a candidate for sainthood. In reality, I was nothing more than what I'd always been—a desperately needy sinner.

The Truth

The great news of the gospel of Christ is that we are not only saved by God's grace, but we are also made holy by God's grace. Philippians 1:6 promises that the same God who began the work of salvation in us will continue it until we get to heaven. Salvation isn't just about being saved from hell; it's also about being saved for heaven. And the moment we embrace faith in Jesus, God's Spirit begins the holy and lifelong work of preparing us for our heavenly home. Sure, there are things we can do to facilitate God's work in us, but that has nothing to do with trying really hard. The reality is that the more we realize we still have a desperate need for God's daily grace, the better off we'll be.

Blessed Brokenness

Jesus' teachings in the Sermon on the Mount (Matthew 5–7, Luke 6) are the clearest description in the Bible of how life on earth is supposed to look for his followers. Jesus painted a picture with undeniable clarity of how different we are to be when compared to the culture around us (think salt and light). He also painted a picture that is impossible for us to make a reality.

Think about it: Who really knows how to love an enemy? And who really wants to? How many of us have conquered lust or never make false promises? Who among us is always willing to go the second mile or to turn the other cheek when our enemies come after us? And as if those aren't hard enough, which of us is perfect like our Father in heaven is perfect (see Matt. 5:48)? Even if we're confused enough to think we can do some of the things Jesus taught in his sermon, his command for us to be perfect is surely the deal breaker.

Remember who was in the audience when Jesus gave this message. It wasn't just his disciples. The Pharisees were listening too. Jesus basically told the world champions of the try-harder mentality that they weren't doing enough. He raised the bar so high that even they had to realize that they could never attain it. And that was Jesus' point: if you're going to be like God, it's going to come from his best efforts, not yours.

The Sermon on the Mount is Jesus' longest discourse in the Bible and the most detailed teaching he gave us on kingdom living. All that's in the Sermon on the Mount is introduced, at least in concept, in the Beatitudes (Matt. 5:3–12). With one verse—the first verse of both the Beatitudes and the Sermon on the Mount—Jesus launched a spiritual revolution that is still going on today. Do you remember what Jesus said in Matthew 5:3? "Blessed are the poor in spirit, for theirs is the kingdom of heaven."

No statement could have been more radical or counterintuitive for Jesus' audience. For centuries they had been taught that righteousness came by having a spiritual résumé that impressed God—that if they did enough of the right stuff, God would be impressed and pleased. But Jesus taught just the opposite. In one simple sentence—just twelve Greek words—Jesus sent a shot across the bow of all who promoted the try-harder mind-set and forever changed the rules of how we are to approach God: "Blessed are the poor in spirit, for theirs is the kingdom of heaven."

What does it mean to be poor in spirit? Well, what does it mean to be poor? Think about the world Jesus lived in. Poverty was everywhere. It's true that there were some who had managed to become wealthy, but the average person who lived in first-century Palestine survived hand to mouth. Beggars were everywhere. They would hold up their hands and plead for a gift—a scrap of food, a piece of clothing, anything—that might help keep them alive another day. They were completely dependent on someone else for their day-to-day sustenance.

As repulsive as the image of a dependent beggar may be to those of us in our can-do culture, that is precisely the image Jesus chose in order to introduce the message of his kingdom. But he wasn't talking about physical poverty as much as he was spiritual poverty—poor *in spirit*. Jesus taught that the people who were most likely to find God's grace and anointing on their lives were not those who thought they had everything together, but those who knew they didn't.

Jesus basically said that if you feel like a beggar spiritually, if you know there is nothing you can do on your own to honor God, and if you realize that without a major provision of grace from the Father, your attempts at living a God-honoring life will be disastrous, then you are at the starting point of kingdom living. Becoming holy like God and living a true kingdom life is possible only for those who know they can't do it on their own, not those who think they can. That's why Jesus' "poor in spirit" descriptor is often referred to as *brokenness*—unless you're truly broken before God, you will never really experience his love or power in your life.

Dependent, Not Committed

At about the same time I was having my legalism-induced breakdown, God introduced me to a man named Dave Busby. Dave was a well-known preacher who traveled all over the

United States and Europe sharing the message of God's grace. I ran into Dave at a few events, got to know him, and was fortunate to call him a friend. Dave had a wickedly funny sense of humor, and his messages were highly entertaining. But they were also powerful—or, better, anointed.

Dave was diagnosed with polio as an infant. One hip was higher than the other, which made him walk with an awkward gait. He also suffered from heart disease, liver disease, diabetes, and cystic fibrosis. Dave's lungs were about 90 percent dead, so he had a terrible time breathing. On the outside, Dave was a weak shell of a man. But he was one of the godliest men I've ever known and by far the most powerful preacher of the gospel I've ever met. Today he lives in heaven.

God used Dave to help me begin to see the difference between the try-harder mind-set and living out of spiritual brokenness. You see, Dave couldn't try hard. He was doing good to just walk, talk, and stay alive. Being a spiritual perfectionist and having a great spiritual résumé just wasn't an option for him. So he had to beg. He had to go daily before God and plead with him for the anointing and grace to do all that God had for him, because there was no way Dave could do anything on his own to impress him.

Dave used to talk about the difference between *achieved* righteousness and *received* righteousness. Achieved righteousness is what the Try Harder Club thrives on. It's what Jesus rebuked in the Pharisees and condemned as being inauthentic and insufficient. Achieved righteousness is doing the best you can to be holy and then bragging about it. It's superficial and temporary, and it doesn't get you one step closer to God.

Received righteousness is what the poor in spirit have. It is a gift from God. It flows down from the Father and not up through the hard work of the sinner. Received righteousness is the holiness of Christ extended by grace to any who ask for it. It's not just the grace to be saved but the grace to live righteously because you are saved.

God used Dave Busby to help me see the hypocrisy of my own attempts at achieving righteousness. During one particular church service where Dave was preaching, all my sin and failed attempts at pleasing God flashed before my eyes. I had been a Christian for nearly twenty years at that point, and I was a seminary-educated pastor of a church. But I was a complete failure spiritually and a total hypocrite. During Dave's talk, all that guilt and shame came pouring out. I was crying so hard that people around me started to stare. I was shattered, completely broken. In one frozen moment of time, God showed me how upside-down my theology was. I was trying really hard and getting nowhere. I was committed to a cause but completely fruitless and ineffective.

I excused myself from the service and, like Peter when he denied Jesus, went outside and wept bitterly (see Luke 22:62). Later, when I was somewhat more composed, I went and found Dave. We didn't really have a conversation. I didn't need or want one. But I did need to say out loud what I was feeling. So I walked up and whispered in Dave's ear, "Today, I am no longer a committed Christian. I am a dependent Christian."

The difference between the two was now irreversibly clear for me. In all my commitment to Jesus and his cause, I had never learned to lean on him. I had never learned to come to him and drink from the springs of his living waters. I was beginning to see that, like Dave, I needed God's grace to live every day for him. I needed a daily gift. I was as weak and desperate before God as Dave was, I just didn't know it.

That was the turning point for me. I repented of my useless attempts to achieve righteousness, and I embraced the gift of spiritual brokenness. I built into my life the daily, sometimes moment-by-moment practice of seeking the presence and power of God in my life. I learned to turn my hands palms up in prayer as an outward sign of my inward desperation. In the language of King David, I ceased striving and started relishing in the reign of God (see Ps. 46:10 NASB). I began asking God for the filling of his Spirit (see Eph. 5:18). Soon after, my spiritual joy returned, I began to see real fruit in my life, and my desire for the secret sins evaporated.

Raise Your Sails

Consider the example of two boats. Both set out to cross a lake at the same time. One is a sailboat, the other a rowboat. The rowboat gets off to a quick start as its pilot sets a furious pace with his rowing. The sailboat moves a little slower as its pilot raises the sails and waits for the wind. Soon the wind begins to blow steadily and the sailboat moves rapidly past the rowboat. In an hour, the sailboat is miles beyond the rowboat, and yet the pilot of the rowboat has worked much harder. The difference? Wind.

Now consider the Christian life. Some Christians, after receiving their salvation, set out to live the best life they can. They have some good days and bad, but they never really seem to pick up any spiritual momentum. Others seek the anointing and favor of God's Spirit in their lives on a moment-by-moment basis. They ask for his filling and guidance. They pray for the grace to live and love each day as Christ himself would. At the end of a decade, the second group of believers appears to be more Christlike and is bearing significantly more fruit than the first group. What's the difference? God's Spirit. One group wasn't depending on him, one was.

Remember what Jesus told Nicodemus, a Pharisee and a charter member of the try-harder club, in John 3. He said Christians are like the wind—they move as and when God's Spirit guides them (see v. 8).

Are you rowing or waiting for the wind? Are you spiritually exhausted or spiritually refreshed? Is your hope for righteousness in your best efforts or in God's Spirit? As a former member of the try-harder club, I can tell you that the wind of God's Spirit is worth the wait.

Come to Me, All You Who Are Weary and Burdened

Are you exhausted from trying so hard? Are you frustrated that your best efforts produce so little spiritual fruit? Are you condemned by your own hypocrisy? It's time for you to be still and let God take over the work of making you holy. It's time for you to trade the yoke of your achieved righteousness for the yoke of his received righteousness. It's time to embrace your brokenness and spiritual poverty and to confess that you still need him. You always will.

Small Group Discussion Questions

1. What is the try-harder approach to Christian living? Define it in your own words.
2. Turn to the section in the chapter entitled "Blessed Are Those Who Try Really Hard" and reread the description of Clyde the Christian. Do you know any Christians like that? Have you ever felt like Clyde? What area in your life do you feel completely frustrated in regarding your efforts to become godlier?
3. Read Galatians 3:1–5. How do you think the members of the Galatian church felt when they heard those words? How might they have reacted? Now read the passage again but address it to your small group. Change the words and add examples that are relevant to your setting today. What do you think the core of Paul's message is to Christians in Galatians 3:1–5?
4. Read Matthew 5:3. Go around the group and take turns restating it in your own words. See if you can come up with a group translation for it.
5. Why did Jesus promise the kingdom of God to the poor in spirit? What does spiritual poverty have to do with God's kingdom?
6. Why is being a spiritual beggar such a foreign or even repulsive concept to us?
7. What are the differences between achieved righteousness and received righteousness?
8. Can you give some examples of Christians you know who live and serve out of their spiritual brokenness? How are their lives different from those of other Christians?

9. What are some things you can do to help facilitate your dependence on God each day? (Be careful here. We're not looking for rules, steps, or lists.) What are some of the spiritual equivalents to raising your sails and waiting for the wind to blow?

10. After reading this chapter, how will you live differently?

8

You Don't Have to Forgive Someone Who Really Hurts You

Susie and I used to be part of a small group with several pastors and their wives. It was a raw and honest group. We talked openly about our marriage strengths and weaknesses and the pressures of being in ministry together.

On one occasion, a pastor named Derrick decided to get quite honest. He shared about a weekend when his wife had been out of town. The pressures of ministry and church leadership had gotten the best of him. He bought a six-pack of beer and consumed most of it in one sitting. It was a major violation of his personal integrity and their collective marriage values. As Derrick shared the story, his wife sat next to him with a horrified look on her face. Derrick noticed her expression and said, "You remember when I told you about this." It was a statement, not a question. The problem was that Derrick only *thought* he had told her. In reality, he hadn't. She was learning about it right then in front of five other pastors and their wives.

To say that all the oxygen left the room in that moment would be an understatement. Derrick's wife turned away from her husband and started crying. Derrick muttered a quiet, "I'm so sorry." And all the rest of us looked for a rock to hide under. It was a terrible, awkward, painful moment.

How do you forgive something like that? Should you? When someone lies to you, betrays your confidence, and then publicly humiliates you, should he be forgiven? Does he deserve to be forgiven? Would you be wiser to keep your guard up with a person like that? So what if he's your spouse or a close friend. He's proven he can't be trusted. To forgive him would be foolish. Right?

The Lie

Forgiveness is overrated. It's not all it's cracked up to be, and it's really only reserved for people who are on a Gandhi-like mission to change the world. But normal people—people who live in the real world—can't afford to forgive. It just sets them up to get hurt again. And besides that, there are just some things that shouldn't be forgiven.

So goes the lie that says we shouldn't forgive everyone. Actually, it's only one of the lies. In reality, there are multiple versions of the "you don't have to forgive" lie. Let me share a few more.

If you forgive them, you're condoning their behavior. This line of thinking goes something like this: "If I forgive Becky, then I might as well be saying that what she did is no big deal. I can't afford to forgive Becky because I don't want her to think I'm condoning her actions." Such reasoning is very common. Forgiveness is hard because it can often feel like we're letting someone off the hook.

If you forgive them, you also have to forget what they did. How many times have you been told that you need to forgive and forget? But who can forget a rape, infidelity, or child abuse? For many of us, forgiveness seems impossible in some cases because we believe we're also required to forget the offense.

If you forgive them, you're going to have to restore the relationship as well. If forgiveness requires us to be friends with or start spending time with the offender, then forget it. We may never want to see that person again, much less hang out with him or her. And besides that, some of the people we need to forgive may have already died. We can't restore the relationship. So I guess that makes forgiveness impossible in some cases. Right?

Consider Karen. Her husband lied about how he was spending their money, how much debt they had, and how much financial trouble they were really in. She had no idea until he confessed it to her. They were able to borrow some money from her parents and set things right. *And then he did it again*—the lies, the spending, everything. Should Karen forgive him? Wouldn't that be irresponsible? Doesn't God give you a pass on forgiving others when the offense is really bad?

The Truth

Forgiveness is one of the sweetest gifts one human can give to another. It's a mental, emotional, and volitional act of grace that may be unmatched in its breathtaking implications for the life of both the offender and the forgiver. And for Christians, it isn't optional. Jesus requires us to forgive all who wrong us, no matter how significant or frequent the offense.

The Beauty of Forgiving

"I'm going to have to forgive you. I can't keep living like this." Tears streamed down Katherine's reddened cheeks as she spoke. "I don't want to, but I have to. Holding this grudge over your head isn't doing me any good. There's no way you can ever restore what you've taken from me. There's no way you can right the wrong. But I can't live the rest of my life as a victim. I won't go on letting what you did define who I am. So even though you don't deserve it, I forgive you. I'm letting this go. I'm leaving your offense here." Katherine paused for a few long moments, took a deep breath, and then turned and walked away from her father's grave.

When Katherine forgave her father, she was acknowledging that he was incapable of changing what he had done. Her grudge holding wasn't doing her any good. For her own sake, she had to let it go.

Forgiveness, in its purest form, is simply releasing a debt. It acknowledges that someone has wronged us—that a person, through their words, actions, or even inactions, has wounded us. But forgiveness doesn't stop at acknowledging the hurt. It pardons the offender. The forgiving person wisely understands that the offender cannot repay what they have stolen relationally, and that they have no ability to undo the hurt or replace what's been lost. They can only confess their guilt and seek pardon. And that's what forgiveness does—it pardons, it sends the guilt away, it releases the debt.

Besides being a powerful act of obedience, forgiveness also has several positive effects that come with it. Here are just a few.

Forgiveness Heals

Once you decide to forgive, you initiate the healing process. Forgiveness gives your soul permission to move on to the higher and healthier ground of emotional recovery. Forgiveness is to your soul what antibiotics are to infection. It is the curative agent that will help to fully restore your soul. It doesn't immediately remove the pain of the offense, but it does start you on the road to recovery.

I recently had spine surgery. A skilled surgeon cut a small incision in my neck, removed a decaying disk from between my C-4 and C-5 vertebrae, replaced it with a synthetic substance, and then connected the two vertebrae with a small metal plate. I'm in the second month since the surgery, and my back is very sore where the plate is. Why? Because it's healing. The pain tells me that the bone is slowly but surely growing over the plate. It hurts, but it's good. Pretty soon my pain will subside and I'll know I'm healed.

Forgiveness isn't intended to shortcut the healing process. You wouldn't want it to. But forgiveness can and does prevent unnecessary additional pain in your relationships. So go ahead and forgive; it's part of the healing work that God is doing in you.

Forgiveness Frees

Unforgiveness is slavery—not for your offender, but for you. It makes you a captive to the hurt and pain of what happened.

But when you forgive, you declare your independence from the events of the past. Forgiving unlocks the chains of emotional turmoil and relational chaos that accompany grudge holding. Forgiveness is the great liberator of every wounded soul.

Forgiveness Humbles

Pride and entitlement always go with unforgiveness. The longer you hold someone's offense over them, the more likely you are to start feeling arrogant and entitled in your posture toward them. But pride and entitlement never lead to freedom or healing. To move on, you have to humble yourself and let the offense go. Forgiveness is a powerful weapon in the arsenal against thinking too highly of yourself or that you are somehow better than the person who wronged you.

Forgiveness Empowers

It takes real courage and strength to forgive. Anyone can hold a grudge and play the victim, but those who grant forgiveness show a level of personal fortitude that others simply don't have. A man who forgives a wayward wife, a woman who forgives the uncle who molested her as a child, the parents who forgive the drunk driver who ended their son's life—these people all walk with a high level of personal authority and confidence because they rose to the occasion and released someone else's debt. Forgive an offender, and you'll know that with God's help you can do anything.

Forgiveness Models Love

I have a friend here in Austin whose father was brutally murdered several years ago. The assailant was convicted and sentenced to life in prison. My friend did something that I still consider to be one of the greatest, most courageous acts I've ever seen. He drove to the prison where his father's murderer was being held, sat down face-to-face with him, and forgave him. My friend didn't feel like it would do him any good to hold a grudge against his father's killer, even though few people would blame him if he did. Instead, he felt compelled by the Bible to grant this man forgiveness. So he did. He looked directly in the eyes of the man who had killed his father and forgave him. In doing so, he showed that man a level of love that is difficult to find.

Forgiveness is a vivid picture of radical love. It offers something undeserved (forgiveness) to someone who doesn't deserve it (an offender). When you choose to forgive, you're choosing to model the type of love God has for us. You're granting a pardon, not because someone deserves it, but because God has commanded you to. And in doing so, you learn to love the way God does—unconditionally.

How Much Should We Forgive?

One day the disciple Peter approached Jesus with a burning question. He wanted to know just how far the requirement to forgive really went. He asked Jesus, "How many times am I required to forgive someone? Up to seven times?" Peter thought he was big stuff. The rabbis only required a person to forgive three times. Surely Peter's willingness to forgive up to seven times would win Jesus' praise. But Jesus shocked Peter and the other disciples when he responded, "No, Peter, that's not enough. Try seven times seventy." In other words, "If your brother comes to you and genuinely seeks your forgiveness for his sin, no matter how many times he's wronged you and you've forgiven him before, you still forgive him." (See Matt. 18:21–22.)

Jesus' point was that there is no limit to how many times God will forgive us and reengage with us relationally. If God is willing to give us second, third, and any other number of chances, then we must give each other the same.

Why Does Jesus Require Us to Forgive?

Why is forgiveness such a big deal to God? Why doesn't he let us off the hook in the extreme cases? Human nature tells us that there are some offenses that shouldn't be forgiven, but God still requires it. Why?

In short, because he forgives us. In Colossians 3, the apostle Paul wrote, "Therefore, as God's chosen people, holy and dearly loved, clothe yourselves with compassion, kindness, humility, gentleness and patience. Bear with each other and forgive whatever grievances you may have against one another. Forgive as the Lord forgave you. And over all these virtues put on love, which binds them all together in perfect unity" (vv. 12–14).

Did you notice that little six-word sentence in the middle of those verses? "Forgive as the Lord forgave you." How far does forgiveness go? How much are we expected to forgive? Where is the line drawn on what offenses we can refuse to let go of? It's simple: to the degree that God is willing to forgive us, we must forgive others. And the wonderful reality is that God will forgive anything. You can't get so dirty or be so far gone in sin that God won't accept you. He always forgives. And as his forgiven children, we're expected to forgive as well.

Again, it's important to remember that forgiving someone's offense doesn't mean condoning his or her behavior. You can be quite certain that when God forgives us, he isn't condoning our sin. If God were going to just look the other way and act like our sin wasn't an issue, he wouldn't have sent Jesus to die for us. Anyone who has ever participated in a Christian communion service understands the role that acknowledging our sin to God plays in forgiveness. Communion is a vivid recalling of the death of Jesus through the elements of wine and bread. It's a humbling reminder of just what our sin cost Jesus. It tells us that God in no way condoned our transgressions but rather paid the price for them.

Forgiveness can be extended without approving of the offender's actions in any way. That, in part, is why forgiveness is so powerful. It actually places you in a posture of strength and benevolence before the person who has wronged you. When you forgive someone, you declare that you will not remain a victim and that you will not be defined by the offense against you. Besides releasing the debt of your offender and granting grace and mercy to him or her, forgiveness frees you. It delivers you from the tyranny of grudge holding and unrelenting anger.

Exhibit A

Bob and Audrey Meisner were living their dream. They were copastoring a growing church and were cohosts of an internationally known Christian television show. They had three beautiful kids and what appeared to be a very happy marriage. But the curse of busyness hit their marriage, and Audrey found herself not only feeling a little disconnected from Bob but also enjoying the attention of a younger man in their congregation. Before long the two had become emotionally enmeshed, and not long after, the relationship became sexual. Audrey was unfaithful to her husband and put everything they had worked for—their relationship, their family, and their ministry—in jeopardy. After a few weeks, Audrey broke off the affair and confessed her sin to Bob.

How would you respond? What would you do when the person you love and trust most in the world betrays you in an unimaginable way? How can forgiveness even be an option at that point?

Bob and Audrey resigned their respective church and television positions, relocated to a different city, and took refuge in a church where they hoped to begin the healing process. After a few weeks, they discovered that Audrey had gotten pregnant as a result of the affair.

Again, let me ask you: How would you respond? Are there still limits to what you're willing to forgive? Are there some sins that are just so grievous, some offenses that are just so heinous, that you know you could never forgive them? Surely, if there are such deal-breaking sins, Audrey had committed them. Surely she deserved to be publicly exposed and then cast off by her husband, who obviously could do better. Right? What would you do?

Bob didn't divorce Audrey. He didn't cast her off, and he didn't reject the baby she was carrying. By God's grace, and by the power of God's Spirit living in him and loving through him, Bob embraced them both. He forgave Audrey. He helped their children understand the reality of the circumstances surrounding Audrey's pregnancy without shaming or condemning her. Then he began to rebuild and restore his family. And a few months later, when Audrey gave birth to a baby boy, Bob gave the baby his own name: Robert Theodore Meisner.[1]

Ready, Aim, Forgive

Are you ready? Are you ready to take the pressure off your weary soul and forgive? Let's talk about how.

Pray for Perspective

Ask God to give you the fifty-year view of your hurt. When you're in a relational whirlwind of pain, it's easy to lose perspective on the big picture. It's easy to see yourself never moving beyond the grievance. So pray for perspective. As you step toward forgiveness, ask God to show you his point of view. Pray to see your life in twenty, forty, or fifty years. With God's help, you won't see yourself still limping along because of the hurt. Instead, you'll see yourself as whole and free. Ask God to show you his plan for your life down the road. Pray Jeremiah 29:11: "'For I know the plans I have for you,' declares the LORD, 'plans to prosper you and not to harm you, plans to give you hope and a future.'" You'll know that God's desire for you is victory, not victimization.

Fully Weigh and Evaluate the Loss

This is a brutal but important step in the forgiveness process. You can't fully extend forgiveness until you come to grips with the extent to which you've been wronged. In some cases, this won't be too difficult. When a neighbor accidentally mows over your tulips, weighing the full extent of your loss shouldn't take too long or be too involved. In the big scheme of things, your loss isn't too great. But when a spouse has been unfaithful, or when an employer has wrongfully accused you of stealing, or when a former friend is openly slandering you, your hurt and loss are much greater. The temptation in such situations is to skim over just how badly you've been hurt in order to avoid the pain that comes with fully facing the wrong. But if you do that, you're quite likely to miss the healing that comes with forgiveness.

So lean into what's really happened. Don't downplay your loss. If you intend to be completely healed, then you have to fully own what's taken place. I often encourage people to make a list of what their offender's actions have cost them. You do this not to hold it over the offender's head but rather to take full stock of the damages so you can adequately grieve, and then adequately forgive, the offenses.

Fully Extend Forgiveness

Obviously, the most critical step in the forgiveness process is actually freeing your offender from the debt he or she has incurred against you. The process of healing isn't complete until you've looked your offender in the eyes (when possible) and said, "I won't hold this offense against you." Such a moment of pardon is without exception one of the most powerful relational moments you will ever experience.

Come to Me, All You Who Are Weary and Burdened

What grievance are you holding on to? What offender do you still need to forgive? Isn't it time to take on the light yoke of

131

Jesus and release your anger and bitterness? Isn't it time to let God deal with the implications of your offender's sin? It is time for you to forgive them.

Come to Jesus right now and let him heal your wounded and weary soul. Release the debt; forgive the offender. You'll be surprised at how light you will feel and how free you will be.

Small Group Discussion Questions

1. In your own words, define *forgiveness*. Try to be brief and use as few words as possible. Then decide on a working definition of *forgiveness* for your group.
2. Based on your definition, list some of the primary characteristics of forgiveness. What are the most common themes or components that are part of the forgiveness process?
3. Briefly answer the following. Try to get every group member to answer.

    Why is forgiveness so hard?

    Why are we often hesitant to forgive?

    How might forgiving someone be misinterpreted by him or her?
4. Based on this chapter, what are the advantages of forgiving? Why is it so important for us to forgive others?
5. What's the most important thing that forgiveness teaches us about ourselves?
6. If you can't forgive someone or if you don't really want to, what would be a good first step you could take to increase your forgiving spirit?
7. Is there someone you need to forgive? If so, what are you going to do about it?
8. After reading this chapter, how will you live differently?

9

You Missed My Will
for Your Life

Have you ever made a wrong turn?

When my son was about ten years old, I took him on his first real hike up above timberline in the Colorado Rockies. We climbed a relatively easy mountain called Flat Top. We had a great time and even threw in a trip down a beautiful snowy glacier just for fun. On our way down, we bumped into two male twentysomethings from Germany who spoke very little English. Through their broken English and my even more broken German, we figured out that they had quit their jobs, bought as much camping and hiking gear as they could, and made their way to the United States, and they were now spending all summer hiking across the United States and Canada. They had no idea how they were going to get back to Germany, but at the moment, they weren't too worried about it.

Since they weren't familiar with the trails and terrain of the Front Range of the Rockies, they asked if my son and I could lead them down from the glacier and back to the main trail. Being the benevolent hike master that I am and loving the strokes my ego was getting from leading these two young, buff foreigners down a mountain, I quickly agreed.

Just below the glacier but still well above timberline, the descent gets pretty treacherous. Loose rock, snow, slush, running water, and some steep angles make for potentially hazardous hiking. Added to all of this, making the footing even more challenging, is what I call ground cover. Mountain ground cover is basically a low-lying, brushlike plant that grows right at timberline. The air is not thick enough for it to grow tall, so it typically only grows to a couple of feet aboveground. But it's thick and terribly difficult to navigate through. It covers the ground like a solid green blanket and can make seeing and following a trail nearly impossible.

So there I was, leading my son and these two German guys down this treacherous mountain terrain. I was moving along pretty fast, and I was thinking, quite honestly, *I'm pretty cool because I'm doing this.* You know, I was leading my son (we were having a father-son moment), and I was leading these guys from another country (they were no doubt thinking how lucky they were to have met up with this mountain expert). This was pretty cool.

As I was cruising along, I noticed the trail turned suddenly to the right, dropped down a few feet, and then disappeared into some ground cover. Without much thought, I followed it to the right, down a few steps, and into the ground cover. Typically, a trail won't take you through more than two or three feet of ground cover. If the cover is too thick, the trail will simply take you around it. Because the trail disappeared into the ground cover, I assumed that I would take a few steps and be out of it.

I was probably ten or fifteen feet ahead of the three other guys when I charged right into the ground cover and stepped off a rock—and into thin air. I suddenly found myself hanging about sixty feet above the rocks below me. I looked and felt very much like the coyote in the old Road Runner cartoons after he has run off a sheer cliff and is hanging on to a thin branch . . . just before he falls. By God's grace I was able to grab a couple of other branches, put my feet against the wall, and scramble my way back up to the edge. And just about the time I pulled myself up over the ledge, out of harm's way, with my life still flashing before my eyes and my heart pounding in my chest, one of the buff German boys walked up, saw me scrambling up over the ledge, and asked in a thick German accent, "Vrong vay?"

Uh, yeah, you could say that.

Where He Leads Me, I Will Follow

Have you ever taken a wrong turn? I don't mean in hiking or in driving a car, although those can obviously be very costly. I mean in life. Did you go to the wrong college, take the wrong job, choose the wrong major, move to the wrong city, put your kids in the wrong school, or marry the wrong person? If you're human, then you probably have missed a turn or two. I know I have. Even with the best of intentions of seeking and following the will of God, we still veer off course and go our own way.

And to make matters worse, we sometimes take others with us. Maybe you packed your family up and moved them across the city or across the country, only to determine when you got there that it was a bad idea. Maybe you talked some friends into investing in a business with you, only to have all of you lose your money. As a pastor of a church, I deal daily with the pressure of not wanting to lead my congregation off a cliff somewhere—something I am quite capable of doing.

What happens when we miss a turn? What happens when we make a bad decision and miss the will of God for our lives? Is God's will so specific, so fixed ahead of time, that if we miss a page or two of the script, then we can never recover? Is there any wiggle room in God's plans for us?

The Lie

God loves you and has a wonderful plan for your life, but if you miss a step, you're on your own.

That's the way this lie sounds to most Christians. It affirms God's great hopes and dreams for us, but it also warns us that if we stray, those hopes and dreams are lost forever. God simply doesn't have time to be constantly editing our life scripts. You can either follow his or follow yours, but don't ask him to adjust his plan for you because you make bad decisions.

Here are just a few of the most common areas where Christians fear they've missed God's will:

Marriage. What if I married the wrong person? This assumes that God has one specific person picked out for you to marry. If you miss him or her, then it's Plan B (or worse) for the rest of your life.

Career. You really wanted to teach school, but your dad convinced you to get a job that had more earning power. So you became a lawyer. You love the income and know you're having an impact, but you fear that God won't bless you as much because you aren't teaching.

Location. You had the option to take good jobs in two different cities, and both had perks. One had a better community feel—schools, churches, and so on. The other offered a little higher salary. You made the call to move to the town with the better community. Your family is happy, but finances are tight. Now you're second-guessing and wondering if you missed God's will.

Failure. When you were a senior in high school, you gave away your virginity. You had sex only one time and you've been pure ever since. Now, twelve years later, you're engaged. You want to feel happy, but you can't help wondering if you've had to settle in your choice of husbands because you're no longer a virgin. And besides that, are you really qualified to wear white at your wedding? You obviously stepped out of God's will. Why should you act pure when you're not?

These are just a few of the areas where we worry that we've missed God's will. I'm sure you could name others. And with the fear of missing God is also the fear of never getting back to where we're supposed to be. The lie of the "wrong turn" is that once we've stepped off the ledge, we can never get back to safety. Once we miss God's plan, we will always be living with second best.

The Truth

Seeking and doing God's will isn't a pass/fail proposition. It isn't an exact science and we're not always going to get it right.

138

If God had wanted to, he could have given us instructions in his Word that were much more specific about discerning his will. But he didn't. He told us to delight ourselves in him and to seek first his kingdom. Jesus seemed content to describe God's will as believing in him. Beyond that, he didn't say much about it.

There's no doubt that Jesus knew God had specific plans for his life. Jesus lived his life in perfect harmony with God and never missed an assignment. But we're not as discerning as Jesus, and neither are we perfect. We're going to miss it sometimes, and when we do, God's grace prevails.

The Grace Net

The famous Golden Gate Bridge in San Francisco was built between 1933 and 1937, during the Great Depression. It was quite an ambitious undertaking for the times, and jobs on the bridge's construction crew were highly sought after. They were also highly dangerous. Rain, fog, and high winds made the work treacherous. Workers frequently slipped on the slick steel or were simply picked up by the strong winds and carried off the bridge. Dozens of workers fell several hundred feet to their deaths in the early years of the bridge's construction. Because of the danger and the tentativeness of the men on the bridge, work slowed dramatically. The conditions were just too dicey for the workers to feel comfortable.

To increase safety, the construction company's engineers designed and created a massive net that they suspended under the bridge. It was several feet wider than the bridge and equally as long. If a worker fell, he had a really good chance of landing in the net and living to tell about it.

The net was successful in doing its job. With the fear of falling gone, morale and the speed of work picked up dramatically on the bridge.

Following God and seeking his will is like working on a high bridge. Sometimes we're going to misstep and fall. But under us is God's net of grace. He will catch us. God doesn't want us to live timid Christian lives. He wants us to live with a sense of passion and boldness. If we spend our days trying to avoid the land mines of stepping out of God's will, then we'll be afraid to take any risks for his kingdom. But when you know there is a net of grace, when you know that God will catch you and set you back on his path when you fall, then you'll feel the freedom to pursue the adventure that kingdom living is all about.

God's promise of grace is not an invitation to recklessness but to fearlessness.

Exhibit A

In Acts 16, the writer Luke tells us that the apostle Paul was all over the map, literally. He was trying to discern God's will and the direction he was supposed to travel in his missionary endeavors. Keep in mind that travel in Paul's day was much more arduous than in ours. He couldn't just turn the car around or catch the next plane to wherever. Mistakes and misfires meant wasted time, energy, and resources. They could also cause those he was trying to lead to question his wisdom.

Below is Luke's account of the efforts of Paul's team to figure out where they were supposed to go. I've added my own comments in brackets:

Paul and his companions traveled throughout the region of Phrygia [250 miles northwest of Derbe and Lystra, v. 1] and Galatia [50 miles northeast], having been kept by the Holy Spirit from preaching the word in the province of Asia [further northeast]. When they came to the border of Mysia [300 miles to the west], they tried to enter Bithynia [north], but the Spirit of Jesus would not allow them to. So they passed by Mysia and went down to Troas [75 miles southwest]. During the night Paul had a vision of a man of Macedonia standing and begging him, "Come over to Macedonia and help us." After Paul had seen the vision, we got ready at once to leave for Macedonia [50 miles northwest by boat], concluding that God had called us to preach the gospel to them. (Acts 16:6–10)

I find that to be a fascinating and strangely comforting piece of Scripture. It shows us that even the strongest, most dedicated believers can't always easily discern what God's specific will is in a matter. And while Paul and his team were bouncing around the map trying to figure out where they should go, God wasn't casting them aside because they didn't get it right on the first try. They fell into God's net of grace, and he caught them, set them back on their feet, and helped them find their way.

Later, after Paul sailed to Macedonia, he led his team eighty miles to the north to the little Roman colony of Philippi. There he met a wealthy woman named Lydia. Lydia and her entire family came to faith in Christ through Paul's testimony, and she started a church in her home. Philippi would later become a stronghold for the Christian faith in the midst of the dark and perverse Roman culture. And several years later Paul would write a letter to all the Christians in the city of Philippi. It would become known as the "epistle of joy" because of its beautiful and encouraging message to the Christians in that city. The New Testament book of Philippians is that letter.

Whatever mistakes Paul made in his efforts to find God's will, it's obvious that God helped him overcome them. For all his misfires, Paul finally landed in exactly the right spot in Philippi. I imagine that Philippi was nowhere on Paul's radar when he set out on his journey. But God was patient with him and guided him, even through all his starts and stops, to the right destination. The result was that a very strategic Roman colony was ambushed by the gospel of Jesus.

Do you feel like Paul? Do you feel like you're all over the map trying to figure out what God wants? Don't fret over it. Stay patient, humble, and prayerful. God will help you find your way.

On the Road Again

This is embarrassing to admit, but I'm pretty sure I took a major wrong turn in my life and stepped out of God's will for at least three years. But this story isn't about my wrong turn; rather, it's about God's grace.

I helped plant a church in Austin in April of 1985. Before it launched, I spent most of 1984 knocking on doors in the neighborhood and leading a Bible study. Susie and I served at that church until September of 1989, and I was a young, inexperienced pastor when I started it. While we saw much growth and blessing from God for the five years we were there, we also saw some severe trials. My young and inexperienced leadership style didn't mingle too well with the seasoned leadership of some of the church's deacons. We started off well but ended up clashing terribly. It was a painful time.

The years 1987 and 1988 were especially rough. So rough, in fact, that I got physically sick. I developed a stomach ulcer that I still feel today on occasion. I lost several pounds, couldn't eat or sleep, and felt very much alone. Those long eighteen months hurt my marriage, my ministry, and my relationship with Jesus. Bottom line—by the end of 1989, I was exhausted.

The crisis ended when all of the families with whom I had been in conflict left the church. Finally, we had peace. Our worship services were filled with joy, our business meetings were more than civil, and it felt like revival had come to our church. But the damage had been done—I was spent.

I was about to graduate with my master's degree, and I was looking at starting a doctorate. I was attending school in Fort Worth and had been commuting while doing my master's work. In August of 1989, I traveled to Fort Worth to look into the doctoral program. I sat down with several professors and told them what I was thinking about doing. One of them, I think it was the last one I talked to, told me I should move to Fort Worth. He said I would do much better in the program there than if I lived in another city. He encouraged me to leave my church, move to Fort Worth, and focus on my studies.

I went back to Austin and told Susie that I needed to resign, and I did so in front of our stunned congregation just a few days later. In September, I preached my last sermon as pastor of the church and started my doctoral studies the next day. I drove to Fort Worth and back from Austin (about 185 miles) four days a week, from September to December. Finally, my family moved to Fort Worth in January of 1990. And the whole thing was probably wrong.

Looking back, I think I resigned out of sheer exhaustion. Susie and I had never really discussed if or when we should leave that church, and we certainly hadn't prayed about it. When that well-meaning professor encouraged me to move to Fort Worth, he gave me the out I had been subconsciously looking for. Being a pastor had chewed me up and spit me out. What I saw was a chance to run away from a hard assignment and still look spiritual and even academic in the process. I mean, it's hard to argue with a guy who wants to better his education and pursue another degree of higher learning. It all looked and sounded really good.

There was just one problem—it wasn't God's will.

I'll never forget the day after I resigned. I was sitting alone at a lunch table at the seminary. I didn't know anyone. I had just completed my first of countless three-hour, twice-a-day trips on I-35. As I sat there eating my bologna sandwich and Cheetos, I reflected on the last fourteen whirlwind days. In that time, I had gone from being a pastor who had sweated, bled, prayed, and fought for a church I loved dearly, living in a city I loved equally as much, to being an unemployed, first-semester doctoral student in a city where I knew no one. We had no place to live in Fort Worth and no plan. Susie and I had one child, and she was expecting our second in three months. I remember having this terrible feeling—*Oh, dear God, what have I done?*

Can you relate? Have you ever had one of those "Oh, dear God, what have I done?" moments? The great news about following Christ is that you can't get so far out of God's will that he won't meet you where you are. Grace still applies. He will find you and lead you back to where you're supposed to be.

Today, Susie and I know that we are 100 percent in the middle of God's will. We have no doubt that our lives and respective ministries here in Austin are exactly what God has planned for us. But I'm still not sure how he got us back on track. I definitely believe that when we left Austin in 1989, it was premature. But somewhere along the line, God regained our attention, redirected our paths, and, as in the example of Paul, took us to "Philippi." We've had more impact, more joy, and far more favor on our lives and ministries than we ever dreamed possible. We still don't know how and when God got us back on his path, but we're sure he did.

Come to Me, All You Who Are Weary and Burdened

Did you miss God's plan somewhere along the way? Have you stepped out of his will? Don't panic. There is a huge net of grace under you. God can and will restore you to his path. He can make good out of any situation. He can and will meet you where you are and transform your situation from bad to good, from painful to glorious.

It's time to release the yoke of guilt for having missed God's will and the fear that you can never regain the ground you've lost. It's time to set aside the heavy yoke that sees God as punitive and uncaring. He knows you're going to misstep and make poor decisions. Those aren't deal breakers for God. He has grace for those who have wandered off course, no matter how far.

Pick up Jesus' yoke of grace today. Take up his yoke of forgiveness, restoration, and redirection. God gave his Spirit to speak to us, to lead us, and to restore us when we stray. Ask God's Spirit, the wonderful Comforter and Counselor, to guide your steps today. He will guide you home.

Small Group Discussion Questions

1. Can you name a time in your life when you think you missed God's will? What happened? Why do you think you weren't doing what God wanted you to do?

2. The chapter listed several common areas where Christians feel they've missed God's will—marriage, career, location, and moral failure. There are obviously many more. Do you think any of your family or Christian friends may have missed God in one of these areas? What about you? Could you relate to any of these? What other common areas of missing God's will could we list?

3. "Seeking and doing God's will isn't a pass/fail proposition. It isn't an exact science and we're not always going to get it right. If God had wanted to, he could have given us instructions in his Word that were much more specific about discerning his will. But he didn't. He told us to delight ourselves in him and to seek first his kingdom." As you read those sentences in the chapter, how did they make you feel? Did they encourage you? Why do you think God didn't give us more instruction on how to know his will?

4. Read Matthew 6:33. What does this teaching of Jesus have to do with how we discover God's will in a specific matter?

5. Recount the story of the net under the Golden Gate Bridge. As the author talked about God's net of grace, how did it make you feel?

6. What is the difference between being reckless and being fearless in trying to follow God?

7. Read Acts 16:6–10. What did you learn about Paul as he struggled to find out where God wanted him to go? How did God finally make his will clear to Paul? What does this passage teach us about how God leads us?

8. In the author's personal story, he suggested that he was wrong to leave his church so soon. He felt that his resignation and subsequent move to Fort Worth were not part of God's will for him and his family. But later he was sure he was now exactly where God wanted him. What hope can you gain and what lessons can you learn from his story?

9. Do you have a yoke of guilt or fear that you've missed God's will for your life? What would be required for you to give it to Jesus?

10. After reading this chapter, how will you live differently?

10

I've Given Up on You

It's called *unadoption*—the process by which a couple dissolves the adoption of their son or daughter. It's a growing trend among adoptive families. Few situations are sadder or more tragic.

There are many reasons an adoption might dissolve. In some rare cases, the adopted child, perhaps as young as fourteen, will petition a court to reverse his or her adoption. More often, however, adoptions are dissolved at the request of the parents, usually after they have discovered their adopted son or daughter has significant preexisting medical or emotional health issues that, in turn, create more strain than they can manage as a family.[2] In other words, unadoption happens when the adoptive parents determine that the child they brought into their home isn't what they were hoping for.

Consider the tragic case of Helen, a fifty-seven-year-old Virginia woman. She adopted her son Toby when he was nine. He had lived in foster homes since he was sixteen months old, had been abused by his biological parents, and was most likely bipolar. Helen claims she found out about Toby's difficult upbringing and health issues only after she had adopted him. She wants to sever the relationship, but Toby is now fifteen and a state law requires that he give his consent before he can be removed from his home and the adoption dissolved. Curiously and even more tragically, Toby still wants to remain with his mother.[3]

What's an adopted child to do when his parents no longer want him?

The Heavenly (Former) Father

Now consider Diane. Diane is a thirty-eight-year-old divorced mother of two. She grew up in church and was active in her youth group through high school. But like many of her friends, she stopped going to church in her college years. The pull of late Saturday night parties and a newfound lifestyle that often left her feeling guilty about her decisions were more than enough to make church an inconvenient option. Diane didn't stop believing, but she stopped acting like a believer.

Diane married her college sweetheart but later went through a divorce she didn't really want. There was no scandal; her husband just grew tired of her and wanted more. He left Diane with two young kids, a mortgage, and no career skills or experience to speak of.

Diane's mother has been encouraging her to go back to church. She keeps telling her that besides the encouragement she would get in her parenting, she might just meet a good man there. But Diane, at least so far, has no interest in returning to church. Why would she? She hasn't read her Bible in years, prays only occasionally, and really isn't sure what she believes anymore.

But beyond that, there's a deeper reason Diane won't go back to church. She's pretty sure God is done with her. She may have been a Christian when she was a kid, but that was a long time ago. She's been to too many parties, slept with too many guys, and failed in too many areas to ever be considered a Christian.

Diane knows that God has his standards. Whatever they are, she's quite sure she slid well below them years ago. Even if Diane wanted to consider herself a Christian, she knows that God will no longer have her.

The Lie

God is done with you. You've strayed too far. You once were his child, but you've broken his heart one time too many. He's disavowed his relationship with you. You are no longer a Christian.

That's how this lie sounds, and it's one that many Christians believe. It implies that God used to love you and that you used to be his child. But things have changed. You're no longer worthy of the name *Christian*. God has cast you out. You have fallen from grace.

This is a paralyzing trick of the devil. As long as a believer is worrying about whether or not they are truly saved, they will never grow up in spiritual maturity. It basically guarantees that a Christian will remain stuck in spiritual infancy. And worse, it paints a picture of God that is not only untrue but also unbiblical. It cheapens the gift of salvation—the gift of grace—and makes God look like a finicky human.

Many Christians still believe that salvation can be lost. Preachers still preach it, scholars still write about it, and well-meaning parents still warn their kids about it. "You'd better be careful and you better behave. If you go too far in your sin, God just might write you off—permanently."

The Truth

It is impossible for Christians to lose their salvation. Everything about the nature of salvation argues for its permanency. God doesn't give and then take the gift back; he doesn't adopt and then unadopt.

It is imperative that Christians learn to think biblically on this issue. As long as we believe that we are one bad decision away from being disowned by God, then we will always live in fear and never press on to spiritual maturity (see Heb. 6:1). So let's settle this argument right now. Though I could give you more, here are five biblical reasons why you can't lose your salvation.

1. You Didn't Earn It

The radical, scandalous message of the gospel is that we are saved in spite of ourselves. God granted us salvation because he loves us, not because we did anything to merit his favor. We simply don't and can't earn God's gift of salvation.

Now make sure you get this—*if we can do nothing to earn God's favor, then we can do nothing to lose it either.* You don't stay saved because of your good acts or great faith, you stay saved because God irreversibly saved you.

The Bible makes this fact very clear. In Ephesians 2:4–9, Paul taught that our salvation is based entirely on God's work, not ours. We can't boast in or take credit for our salvation. That's part of the humbling nature of the Christian message. We can't earn it; we can only receive it as a gift. Five times in the book of Acts, salvation is referred to as a gift (1:4; 2:38; 8:20; 10:45; and 11:17). In Acts 8:20, Peter rebuked Simon the sorcerer for thinking that he could purchase the gift of God's Spirit with money. Peter's obvious point is that what God offers us through Jesus is far more valuable than what any amount of money can buy or any religious efforts can merit. Something so valuable can be given only as a gift. It can't be earned or bought.

Why do you give gifts? Because you love someone? Because he or she is valuable to you? Because you're trying to communicate your feelings for him or her? All of those are noble reasons. But they're only mere human reflections of the divine concept of giving. God gives out of perfect love and motives. His gifts are immeasurable and priceless. John 3:16 tells us that God's love for us moved him to give his Son to die, just so we could have the opportunity to believe. Nowhere in the Bible is it even implied that God's gifts come with conditions, are on a trial basis, or can be revoked. In fact, the Bible states just the opposite. In Romans, while discussing God's ongoing relationship with the nation of Israel, Paul reminded the Roman believers that "God's gifts and his call are irrevocable" (11:29).

It cheapens the nature of grace to assume that it is applied to a sinner with a footnote attached. There is no point at which grace depends on the good or bad deeds of a person. That's why you can't lose it—because you didn't earn it in the first place. "And since it is through God's kindness, then it is not by their good works. For in that case, God's grace would not be what it really is—free and undeserved" (Rom. 11:6 NLT).

2. God Initiated It

When you became a Christian, you did so in response to the wooing of God in your life. People who are spiritually dead (see Eph. 2:1–3) don't just go looking for God. They don't even know they need him. When a sinner starts their search for God, they do so in direct response to the stimuli of God in their life—the witness of the Holy Spirit, the revelation of God in nature, or the testimony of a believing friend. God uses these stimuli and others to awaken the spiritual awareness of an unbelieving person. Whenever a sinner crosses the line of faith and believes in Jesus, it's always because God has first drawn them and convicted them.

In John 6:44 Jesus taught, "No one can come to me unless the Father who sent me draws him." Later he reiterated the same point when he said, "This is why I told you that no one can come to me unless the Father has enabled him" (v. 65). His point is that salvation is impossible if it isn't first offered to the sinner by God. If he doesn't draw us, then we'll never have the spiritual sense to look for him.

So why would God woo people to him, accept their prayer of faith, and name them as his followers, only to reject them later? He doesn't do that. He doesn't make mistakes or go back on his word. He woos needy sinners to him with full awareness of their spiritual condition.

If you're a Christian, you are so because God led you to himself and you accepted his invitation to a relationship with him. God won't accept you one day and reject you the next.

He isn't finicky and won't change how he views you, even if you change how you view him.

3. You Have a New Identity

When you became a Christian, God made you a completely different person in Christ. It was an irreversible act. Second Corinthians 5:17 teaches that as believers, we are totally new creations in Christ; we're a completely new species. Our old lives and identities are gone and have been replaced by new ones, permanently. We are neither who nor what we used to be. Our lives are now hidden in Christ (see Col. 3:3).

The entire notion of a new creation implies permanence. In the same way that a butterfly cannot return to the cocoon and revert back to being a caterpillar, men or women who have been given a new identity by God in Christ, whose old selves have been crucified with Jesus, cannot revert to their pre-Jesus nature. It's simply impossible. They may act like they did before becoming a follower, but their nature doesn't change. The river that runs through them is the river of Jesus' blood. It cannot be removed. Their identity is now summed up in Christ.

4. God Promises to Complete His Work in You

The related works of salvation and sanctification in the life of a believer are both the result of grace and God-dependent from start to finish. And what God starts, he always finishes. In Philippians 1:4–6, Paul encouraged the believers in Philippi with that truth. He told them that he always prayed for them with great joy because of their steadfast work in spreading the gospel, and because "he who began a good work in you will carry it on to completion until the day of Christ Jesus" (v. 6). Paul had no fear that God would let up on his work in the Philippian Christians. He knew that what God begins, he always completes.

The same is true for you today. Think back to that time when you knew for certain you believed. At that moment, God began the work of making you holy. He turned his Holy Spirit loose in you and gave him permission to change you into the image of God's Son. His Spirit will not stop that work. He will purge, protect, grow, and reshape you until you get to heaven.

5. God Has Adopted You

The apostle Paul often used the metaphor of adoption when describing a Christian's connection to God. In Paul's culture, adoption was an irreversible action that granted all the rights, privileges, and inheritance of the adopter to the adoptee. Paul took that image and listed adoption as one of the spiritual blessings we have in Christ: "In love he predestined us to be adopted as his sons through Jesus Christ, in accordance with his pleasure and will" (Eph. 1:4–5; see also Rom. 8:23).

Unlike the tragic reversal of adoption that we talked about earlier, God has no such option. He doesn't need it. God adopted you and declared you holy with full knowledge of all your sins and weaknesses. He won't ever change his mind and decide that you're no longer worthy to be called his child. It's the fact that you weren't worthy to begin with and he chose to adopt you anyway that guarantees your security as his child now.

The prophet Isaiah called God the eternal Father (see Isa. 9:6). That doesn't just mean that God is the Father who exists forever; it means that he is your Father forever. He will never stop being your heavenly, eternal Father.

These are five great reasons to rest in the fact that God will not cast you away as a Christian. He may discipline, prune, and challenge you, but he won't kick you out of his family. What God does can't be undone. What God secures can't be stolen. What God saves can't ever be lost.

Exhibit A

Consider the moving example of the prodigal son in Luke 15. I love that story because I can so easily relate to it. A son born to a man of wealth takes his inheritance and moves away, then blows the inheritance on wild living. He totally disgraces his father's name and the legacy his father had given him. But when he finally does return home, his father greets him with open arms. Even in all of his wild living and rebelliousness, he had never ceased to be his father's son.

In the parable, the father represents God. The wayward son could represent any of us who have pushed away from our faith and blown our spiritual inheritance on wild living. I certainly did. I made multiple poor choices and was wild enough to make everyone who knew me question if I had ever known God. For over three years, nothing in me resembled a Christian.

Can you relate? You could be the philosophy major who went through a long period of doubting God's existence. Or you could be the woman who had an abortion in high school and never told anyone. You may be the guy who, even after growing up in church, developed a cocaine habit that eventually cost you your job and marriage. Or you could be the woman who got turned off by all the hypocrisy in church, stopped going, and eventually lost your faith.

Prodigal sons and daughters come in all shapes and sizes, and they all have their own sordid tale to tell. But the parable is about the prodigal *son*—not the *former son*, the *ex-son*, or the *sinner formerly known as a son*. Prodigals, even on their worst days, are still sons or daughters. They may wander from God, but they never cease being his child. That's the point of the story of the prodigal son. He came back, and his father welcomed him immediately. If and when you have strayed, if you have the courage to repent and turn back to God, he will welcome you as well.

Why Don't I Feel Like a Christian?

Many Christians doubt their salvation because they don't feel as close to God as they used to. They feel like their prayers bounce off the ceiling and that they don't have any real intimacy with God. They often and incorrectly conclude that they must have strayed away from God at some point and that he has written them off. I can't tell you the number of people I meet who live with this oppressive theological uncertainty. But in reality, something else is going on, and it's something that can be easily fixed.

People who don't feel like they're still Christians are typically Christians who are out of fellowship with God. Their stories are amazingly similar. For whatever reason—they moved to a new city, they had a falling-out with church friends, they have young children—they stopped going to church. They aren't being fed spiritually and typically don't

157

have any close Christian friends. They've plateaued spiritually and aren't growing. Beyond that, in the absence of good spiritual feeding, sin has crept in. And as a result, they just don't feel God's presence in their lives. They don't sense his favor and don't believe their prayers are being answered.

That's when Satan chimes in with his lies: *You're not a Christian. God has turned away from you. You went one step too far and now you're on your own. He doesn't love you and he'll never have you back.* If you're in a weakened spiritual state, those lies sound very believable and can be devastating. But they're not true.

I've literally seen hundreds of Christians over the years rediscover their relationships with God by simply reengaging in Christian community. When they open their lives up to the fellowship of other believers, they quickly reawaken their sleeping faith and find that God was with them all along. I'm not saying that community is the only necessary step in the repentance and restoration process—far from it. I'm saying that people who feel lost to God can quickly rekindle the flame of their faith by surrounding themselves in authentic Christian relationships. As they do, important spiritual disciplines like prayer, worship, serving, and Bible study follow. And as they mature in their walk with Christ, they quickly move past the stage where they doubted their salvation.

Tyler is a great example. I first met him in our church's membership class, where he shared that he didn't know where he was spiritually and that he was probably an agnostic. When I pressed Tyler for more details, he shared that he had grown up in a nominally Christian home and had been baptized as a child. He had strayed from church in college and quickly found himself wondering if God still loved him. His presence in our membership class, some twenty-five years later, was the first step in his efforts to find out where he was spiritually. Tyler's faith quickly reengaged. He and his wife found their lives completely enmeshed in Christ and the fellowship of his people. Their respective levels of faith took off, and today, nearly six years after I met them, they are both very godly leaders in our church. Tyler now understands that he had never ceased being God's son. He was indeed a prodigal, and all it took was his returning to his Father and his Father's people to kick-start his faith.

What about Those Troubling Passages?

There certainly are some difficult passages in the Bible that could, depending on how they're interpreted, lead one to conclude that it is possible for a Christian to lose his or her salvation. It is not my intention here to address in detail every passage that might be troubling. However, I think I can give you enough context and understanding of the most troubling verses to help you feel comfortable with the fact that they do not teach that a Christian can lose salvation.[4] Following are the verses, and then we'll deal with them one at a time:

> "So I tell you, every sin and blasphemy will be forgiven men, but the blasphemy against the Spirit will not be forgiven. Anyone who speaks a word against the Son of Man will be forgiven, but anyone who speaks against the Holy Spirit will not be forgiven, either in this age or in the age to come" (Matt. 12:31–32).

> "It is impossible for those who have once been enlightened, who have tasted the heavenly gift, who have shared in

the Holy Spirit, who have tasted the goodness of the word of God and the powers of the coming age, if they fall away, to be brought back to repentance, because to their loss they are crucifying the Son of God all over again and subjecting him to public disgrace. Land that drinks in the rain often falling on it and that produces a crop useful to those for whom it is farmed receives the blessing of God. But land that produces thorns and thistles is worthless and is in danger of being cursed. In the end it will be burned" (Heb. 6:4–8).

"If anyone does not remain in me, he is like a branch that is thrown away and withers; such branches are picked up, thrown into the fire and burned" (John 15:6).

"If we endure, we will also reign with him. If we disown him, he will also disown us" (2 Tim. 2:12).

"You who are trying to be justified by law have been alienated from Christ; you have fallen away from grace" (Gal. 5:4).

Matthew 12:31–32. Many believers who have ever doubted God, gotten angry with him, or said things to or about him that they later wish they hadn't often fear that they have committed the "unpardonable sin" and blasphemed the Holy Spirit. While this is certainly a serious teaching from Jesus, it is in no way spoken to Christians as a warning that they might actually blaspheme God's Spirit. That, simply stated, is something a Christian is no longer capable of doing.

To blaspheme the Holy Spirit is to impugn his character; it's to call him a liar. The Spirit testifies to us about the reality of our sin, the validity of Jesus, and our need for him. Those who blaspheme the Spirit are people whose opinions of Jesus call into question or even flatly deny the validity of the Spirit's witness about him. They conclude that Jesus is not God's Son and the Savior of the world, thus rejecting the Spirit's testimony about him. Blaspheming the Spirit is a lifetime sin, not something committed in a moment or even a season of rebellion. A person who is concerned that they have blasphemed the Spirit can be quite certain that they haven't. Those who actually do slander God's Spirit never worry about the implications of doing so.

Hebrews 6:4–8 (see also 10:26–31). The author of Hebrews wrote to Jewish Christians who were thinking of abandoning their Christian faith and returning to Judaism in hopes of avoiding the growing persecution of Jesus' followers. The writer urged them not to, pointing out the emptiness of the Jewish faith without the Messiah (Jesus) and warning them that they would find themselves in a kind of spiritual no-man's-land if they tried to revert to their pre-Christian religion. They would lose their intimacy with Christ, and for what? They would be back in a religion that had now been shown to be incomplete and insufficient without Christ.

If Christians reject their faith and turn to religion and works to save them, they're treading on the blood of Jesus and treating his grace as insignificant. They quench the Spirit's work within them and lose the supernatural favor of God's anointing on their lives. They may actually live out their days on earth feeling like spiritual orphans. Not orphans literally, because God will never forsake them, but they will greatly resemble spiritual runaways who, by rejecting Christ after being saved, create a terrible spiritual reality for themselves in this life that is miserable to say the least—it is very much like a self-imposed exile from God.

Such an outcome for Christians sounds harsh indeed, but it matches the urgency of the warnings given to believers in the book of Hebrews.

It is worth noting that the writer of Hebrews believed his readers would not abandon their faith but would rather stay the course and remain faithful to their Christian calling (see Heb. 6:9). It also must be noted that the writer didn't seem concerned with his readers' eternal security, but rather the severe consequences that would come their way in this life if they abandoned Christianity and reverted back to Judaism.

John 15:6. In this verse, the security of believers is never in question, but rather their fruitfulness. This sounds much like the warning given to the Hebrew Christians referenced above. Jesus was using the metaphor of a gardener and a vine, something familiar to his audience. The point of the metaphor is that, like a branch that stays connected to the vine, Christians can bear fruit only if they stay connected to Jesus. If they don't, they basically become deadweight in the kingdom. Useless branches are cut off and burned. Useless Christians, if they don't repent, will no doubt face God's discipline and have little eternal fruit to speak of.

This teaching also sounds quite similar to Paul's warning to unfruitful Christians in 1 Corinthians 3:10–15. Concerning fruitless Christians, he wrote that their works would be "burned up," they would "suffer loss," and they would be saved, but "only as one escaping through the flames" (v. 15).

Second Timothy 2:12. This is a stern warning to unbelievers in the midst of a beautiful Christian confession. If we choose to honor God, he will honor us. But if we choose to deny him, then he certainly will deny us. Jesus said something similar in Matthew 10:33.

The denying that Paul mentions here is not referencing the day-to-day or even seasonal failures that we all experience in life. Peter denied Jesus, but God did not deny him. Rather, he forgave him, rescued him, and made him into a great leader in his church. The denying that Paul mentions here is the lifetime denial Jesus spoke of when he talked about the unpardonable sin. It's the verdict of a life that renders the Son of God irrelevant and the Holy Spirit a liar. That cumulative denial, God will not forgive.

Galatians 5:4. The phrase "fallen from grace" is frequently used to describe the supposed plight of those who have ceased to believe and have lost their salvation. But this verse has nothing to do with losing one's salvation. Paul's warning here is to those who choose the way of legalism over against the way of grace. If a sinner chooses to rely on his best efforts and religious performance to gain favor with God, then he has rejected the way of grace. Indeed, he has fallen away from it. It is much like one who, while trapped in a burning house, repeatedly rejects the efforts of those trying to save him.

Come to Me, All You Who Are Weary and Burdened

It's time for you to get over this hurdle. It's time to get past wondering if today will be the day that you blow it so badly that God writes you out of his spiritual will. As long as you live in fear that God may reject you at some point, or that he already has, you will never grow into a fruit-bearing Christian. You will always be motivated by fear, not love.

The message of grace that is part and parcel of the gospel is that we are saved and secured in Jesus for free. We can live boldly and with a childlike innocence before God, knowing that we are not going to do everything right as Christians. Grace gives us the freedom to live carefree and spontaneous lives as his followers without the fear of being rejected if and when we fail.

Is carrying the responsibility of your salvation too heavy a yoke for you? Hand it to Jesus. Take on his yoke of love and freedom and let him carry the yoke of your spiritual security. He died so that you could be free from the burden of having to earn his love or approval.

I invite you to set this book down, turn your hands palms up before God, and confess yourself as his permanently adopted child. Today, right now, with all of your sin and insecurities, you're his. And if you've feared that somehow you lost God along the way, know that you are secure. He's been with you all along.

> While he was still a long way off, his father saw him and was filled with compassion for him; he ran to his son, threw his arms around him and kissed him.
>
> The son said to him, "Father, I have sinned against heaven and against you. I am no longer worthy to be called your son."
>
> But the father said to his servants, "Quick! Bring the best robe and put it on him. Put a ring on his finger and sandals on his feet. Bring the fattened calf and kill it. Let's have a feast and celebrate. For this son of mine was dead and is alive again; he was lost and is found." So they began to celebrate. (Luke 15:20–24)

Small Group Discussion Questions

1. Have you ever doubted your salvation or feared that God had disowned you? Why?
2. Why does the devil spend so much time trying to get believers to doubt their salvation? Why is it such an effective trick of his?
3. Read Ephesians 2:1–9. What does it say about the nature of our salvation? What does God do and what do we do?
4. Read John 6:44, 65. What part does the wooing or pull of God play in our ability to seek him?
5. Read 2 Corinthians 5:17 and then restate it in your own words. How would you explain the meaning of this verse to a third-grader?
6. Read Ephesians 1:3–5. What does Paul say about our spiritual blessings and our relationship with God?
7. Why is the story of the prodigal son important for Christians who doubt their salvation?
8. Why is it difficult for us to believe that we are secure in our salvation, even if we don't live good lives? What does the fact of our spiritual security teach us about the nature of grace?
9. After reading this chapter, how will you live differently?

11

This Is a Cross You Must Bear

Let's try an experiment. Wherever you are, stop reading and look around. How far would you have to walk to see a cross? Look at the art on the walls, your jewelry, your key chain. Is there a Bible or a journal nearby?

I tried this experiment as I was writing these words, and I found crosses everywhere. Of course, I'm in my study and I happen to love crosses, so I would expect to find some here. But there's also a large cross standing on the front porch of my house and several more on the walls inside. I have a cross hanging from the rearview mirror in my car and one in my daily prayer journal. I also have one in the notebook I use whenever I speak publicly. In my life, crosses are everywhere.

What about you? My guess is that you didn't have to go too far to find a cross. Even people who don't believe the Christian message find them to be beautiful and meaningful. They're on T-shirts, CD covers, tattoos, and even architecture. For the most part, many in our culture find the cross attractive.

Why is that? Why is the cross beautiful to so many? No doubt it has become a symbol of hope around the world. Even non-Christians see Jesus' death on the cross as a powerful statement of peace and personal sacrifice. The billion-plus people who do follow Christ today obviously see the cross as a reminder of the greatest act of love in history and one of the tools God used for their salvation. Believers and non-believers alike see the cross as perhaps the most universally recognized inspirational symbol in the world.

That being said, I still believe the cross gets a bad rap today because many Christians, without even trying to, associate the cross with a life of suffering and unhappiness. They do so every time they utter seven simple words: "This is a cross I must bear." Sadly, those people often view the Christian life as one of drudgery and second-best living. They feel like they bear one heavy cross after another, hoping to simply endure it all until they can escape to heaven.

I heard this line of reasoning at a recent breakfast. The man I was with was talking about his impatience with discovering God's will. He was eager to serve God fully but having a dif-ficult time figuring out what God wanted. In his waiting on God, he was growing impatient. He looked at me and said, "I guess my impatience with God is just a cross I have to bear."

Really? Do you see the negative picture that paints of God? It makes him look like he's deliberately withholding his will from this guy just so he can suffer a little longer. While I was frustrated that the guy had such poor theology, I was relieved that he hadn't shared his "cross I must bear" mind-set in front of an unbeliever.

While I know that it is not the intention of this guy or others who feel like he does to disparage the message of the cross, the result is the same: many outside of the Christian faith don't want to give up their freedoms, their fun, and even their happiness by becoming Christians. They equate following Jesus with a life of discomfort and joyless living. They associate Christianity with miserable cross bearing, and they've gotten this message from Christians.

The tragedy is that nothing could be further from the biblical truth. We're giving seekers the wrong impression, and we're blaming it on the cross.

The Lie

This is a cross you must bear. Jesus shouldn't have to bear his cross alone. Every Christian has a cross to carry; this is yours. If you're not suffering or unhappy, you're not growing. If you're happy and prospering, you're probably not godly. Suffering and following Jesus go hand in hand. Christianity is a life of drudgery and heartache. Deal with it.

So goes the common thinking that's spawned by the "cross you must bear" philosophy. That's some pretty effective marketing, isn't it? "Hey, come follow Jesus and be miserable the rest of your life!" No wonder Christians have such a bad name in our culture. The sad part is that many followers of Christ actually believe this. They seriously think that the life of faith is a life of misery and unhappiness, that they're selfish and unbiblical to expect to enjoy their Christian walk. They wear their misery on their sleeves and give every person around them the impression that following Jesus is right up there with having a daily root canal—without Novocain. Ready to sign up yet?

The Culprit

Tragically, the cause of this misplaced "cross you must bear" thinking is a statement Jesus made. Actually, that's not true. The culprit isn't the statement he made, but rather the misinterpretation and misapplication of it. Here's what he said in its original context: "If anyone would come after me, he must deny himself and take up his cross and follow me. For whoever wants to save his life will lose it, but whoever loses his life for me will find it. What good will it be for a man if he gains the whole world, yet forfeits his soul? Or what can a man give in exchange for his soul?" (Matt. 16:24–26).

This statement ("take up your cross") has been used to beat up Christians for centuries. On the surface, it seems easy to misinterpret its meaning: Jesus died on a cross, and figuratively speaking, so must we. He suffered, and so should we. We read this verse through the filter of knowing Jesus died on a cross, so we assume that Jesus is saying we each have a cross we must die on as well. For Christians, cross bearing has come to symbolize just about any type of problem in life: a long bout with cancer, a bad marriage, an evil mother-in-law, being overweight, having an unfair boss or loud neighbors, being a Baylor University fan during football season, and so on.

I'm willing to grant that this verse, if it is read alone and out of context, can be a little startling and very humbling. But even taken alone, it doesn't say that Christians are called to a life of cross bearing. When we add in the full teachings of Jesus and understand when and why he said this, the verse becomes a liberating and beautiful invitation of Jesus to live life with him. That's right. This is another of Jesus' "come to me and take my yoke" statements. It's not an invitation to suffering and unhappiness but rather to finding true life.

The Truth

The cross of Christianity represents the greatest gift ever given to humanity. It speaks of a sacrifice already made, of suffering already completed. It does not stand for a life of drudgery and misery but rather a life of victory and freedom. The fact is that Jesus had to bear his cross alone. No one could have shared that burden with him. To suggest otherwise reduces his standing as the unique and holy Son of God and elevates us to something higher than the struggling sinners we are. Jesus bore his cross alone precisely because we couldn't bear it. And now, through his completed work, we don't have to.

Curiously, the cross was not the first emblem identified with Christianity. Early Christians often used the symbols of a dove, an anchor, or a fish to represent their faith. The site of the garden tomb outside of Jerusalem (one of two probable burial sites for Jesus) has an anchor that clearly dates back to the time of Christ etched in the stone next to the tomb's entrance. It's there indicating that early Christians believed that to be the actual site of Jesus' resurrection.

Besides a cross, there are many other powerful images that early followers of Christ could have latched on to as the emblem of their faith. What about a manger, a carpenter's bench, a servant's towel, a cup of wine and bread, a throne, a boat and discarded fishing nets, or even an empty tomb? Any of those would have made beautiful and powerful images to help Christians identify with and celebrate their faith. But none of those ultimately stuck. For whatever reason, Christians in the earliest centuries of the church's history gradually came to agree that the symbol that best represented the message of their faith—a message not of despair and suffering but of hope and victory—was the cross. Let's find out why.

I Have Decided to Follow Jesus

Look again at Matthew 16:24: "If anyone would come after me, he must deny himself and take up his cross and follow me." Remember, we read this verse with the historical advantage of knowing that Jesus died on a cross. But when Jesus first spoke these words, he wasn't in any way identified with the cross. It was simply an ugly tool of Roman execution. It wasn't a religious symbol. It wasn't attractive. But Jesus changed all that. We think crosses are beautiful because Jesus died on one, and then he rose from the dead three days later.

So what did Jesus mean? What did his disciples think he was saying when he told them that his followers had to pick up their crosses and follow him? In Jesus' day, people picked up and carried a cross for only one reason—they were going to die. People associated with crosses had no life left to live. They had no rights, no freedoms, no property, no expectations, no entitlements. A cross meant one thing for the person bearing it—their life was over.

Look at what Jesus said: "Take up your cross and *follow me*." But the crosses that Jesus' followers carry don't kill them. Do Jesus' disciples willingly forfeit their independence? Yes. Do they set aside their rights and privileges? Yes. But Jesus' cross-carrying followers don't *lose* their lives; they *find* them. To underscore his point, Jesus followed his "take up your cross" statement in verse 24 with this promise in verse 25: "For whoever wants to save his life will lose it, but whoever loses his life for me will find it."

That's why it's insulting to Jesus for us to talk about his cross in a negative way. That's why we shouldn't broadcast to our friends and neighbors the false message of the crosses we bear for him—because in our faith-based association with

Jesus, we find our life's greatest purpose and joy. It's certainly not a problem-free life or one without suffering, but it is a life whose sufferings—whatever they may be—are eclipsed by the glory of Christ. It's a life of unparalleled joy, peace, and purpose. It's a life that Jesus called abundant. And we should never, ever sully it by calling it a cross we must bear. If anything, the cross of Jesus is something we *get* to carry, a yoke we *want* to share.

Exhibit A

The apostle Paul would have been embarrassed and probably even a little angry about the amount of whining and complaining Christians today do about their supposed crosses. Paul knew no such shame or despair about his relationship with Jesus' cross. For him, the cross was the center point of history and something he was thrilled and honored to be associated with.

Paul's life with Christ was no easy journey, and he repeatedly suffered for his faith in Christ. But he didn't resent his sufferings or talk about how bad he had it. Rather, he celebrated his close intimacy with Jesus. To the believers in Philippi he wrote, "I want to know Christ and the power of his resurrection and the fellowship of sharing in his sufferings, becoming like him in his death and so, somehow, to attain to the resurrection from the dead" (Phil. 3:10–11).

The cross of Jesus was at the center of Paul's theology and his worldview. He would never have viewed it as the source of his problems or some burden that he was forced to bear. In fact, he bragged about the role of the cross in his life. To the Christians in Galatia he wrote, "May I never boast except in the cross of our Lord Jesus Christ" (Gal. 6:14). Can you imagine a guy with a mind-set like that ever referring to anything in his life as a cross he had to bear? No way.

Here are just a few of the statements Paul made about the cross:

> "We know that our old self was crucified with him so that the body of sin might be done away with, that we should no longer be slaves to sin—because anyone who has died has been freed from sin" (Rom. 6:6–7).

> "Christ did not send me to baptize, but to preach the gospel—not with words of human wisdom, lest the cross of Christ be emptied of its power" (1 Cor. 1:17).

> "I have been crucified with Christ and I no longer live, but Christ lives in me. The life I live in the body, I live by faith in the Son of God, who loved me and gave himself for me" (Gal. 2:20).

> "Those who belong to Christ Jesus have crucified the sinful nature with its passions and desires" (Gal. 5:24).

> "[God's] purpose was to create in himself one new man out of the two, thus making peace, and in this one body to reconcile both of them to God through the cross, by which he put to death their hostility" (Eph. 2:15–16).

As you can see, Paul viewed the cross as the highest point of hope, power, and inspiration in the Christian's life. It was the symbol of the greatest gift God had given to humanity.

In the Crosshairs

Imagine for a minute that Paul lived in our times and was visiting one of our churches. While pouring himself a cup of hot coffee at one of the church's greeting stations, he hears two ladies talking. One is telling the other about her husband's consistently poor behavior. He stays out late partying with his buddies. He doesn't help around the house and rarely affirms her. She's unhappy in her marriage and doesn't see any signs of things getting better. As she empties a couple of packs of Splenda into her coffee, she tells her friend, "It's sad to admit, but I guess this marriage will end up just being a cross I must bear."

Paul turns around and stares at her. She notices his glare. Let's imagine how their interaction might go.

PAUL: Excuse me, but were you talking about the cross?

WOMAN: No, I was talking about my husband.

PAUL: Oh, I thought I heard you mention the cross. I love the cross. I have life through the cross. So when I thought you mentioned it, I got kind of fired up.

WOMAN: Oh, no, I'm sorry. I just used the word *cross*, you know, kind of as a metaphor. I was just telling my friend here about the sorry state of my marriage. For me, it's kind of like Jesus and his cross. It's just my point of suffering.

PAUL: Excuse me? You're comparing your marriage troubles to Jesus' death on the cross? Are you serious?

WOMAN: Well, what I meant is that—

PAUL: The cross is the greatest expression of love in history. It's the source of hope and eternal life for struggling sinners, and it levels the playing field between Jews and Gentiles, rich and poor, slaves and masters, educated and illiterate, men and women. And you dare to compare it to a bad marriage?

WOMAN (starting to retreat): No, no, it's just a figure of spe—

PAUL: Lady, in the name of the Lord Jesus, I call you to repent of your bad theology and sappy thinking. You need to get on your knees right now and beg God for . . .

I'm guessing Paul wouldn't have lasted long in that church. To the divided and distracted church in Corinth, Paul wrote, "I resolved to know nothing while I was with you except Jesus Christ and him crucified" (1 Cor. 2:2). Paul knew that the centrality of the message of Jesus' cross was just what the misguided Corinthian believers needed. For Paul, the cross was to be promoted, not apologized for.

The message of the cross is not one of our own suffering but rather of our new life. It reminds us of the price that has been paid to free us from sin and to give us access to God's kingdom in the here and now. Because Jesus died, we can live boldly and victoriously. Will we suffer? Some will. Will we be persecuted? Maybe. But compared to the suffering of Jesus for us, any discomfort we know in life is light and momentary (see 2 Cor. 4:16–18). The reality is that the cross shields us from the suffering for our sins that we all should have endured. And in the cross we see the heart of God.

The God of the Cross

Not long ago the church I work for changed insurance carriers. I was required to undergo a litany of tests to make sure I was "insurable." On the appointed day, a female twentysomething showed up at my office, portable lab in hand, ready to assault any number of my veins in the name of due diligence. My young guest didn't really look the part of a nurse practitioner; at least, she didn't look how I expected her to. With her hair dyed a bright red, multiple nose and ear piercings, and a thick layer of black clothing, this girl looked like someone who indeed might have had much experience with needles. But my first impression of her proved to be wrong. She was bright, witty, and articulate. I soon found myself at her mercy medically.

It's amazing how allowing someone to poke you with needles can immediately make you feel close to them. Maybe it's just a matter of the physical closeness involved. Think about it: personal space and boundaries fly right out the window when someone is checking your temperature and taking your pulse, your blood pressure, and three vials of your blood. After a while you just sort of feel connected to them.

I decided to take advantage of this intimacy with my new friend and find out where she stood spiritually. After all, I was a pastor and she was in my office taking my blood. The least she could do was indulge my spiritual curiosity. After a few rounds of surface theological banter, I asked her about her view of God. Her answer astounded me. She told me a new version of a story I had heard before that obviously meant a lot to her. She looked me right in the eye and said something like this:

I heard a story once about a man who worked for a train company. He manned a junction booth at an old bridge that crossed over a river. He had to manually operate the rail switches on the dated bridge tracks, otherwise the train was likely to derail and go careening off the bridge.

The man had a preschool-age son who loved to accompany his daddy to work. He was fascinated by trains and enjoyed watching them as they passed by. Sometimes he'd even get to sit in his dad's lap and help operate the switch controls. It was the perfect playground for a little boy.

One day the boy was standing down by the river when a train was approaching the bridge. As the boy took a few steps out so he could better see the train, he tripped and tumbled headlong into the swirling waters. His father, seated in the control booth, saw the accident and knew immediately that he had only a few seconds to act before his son would be out of reach. He also knew with gut-wrenching clarity that he could not retrieve his son and get back to the booth in time to secure the train's safe passage over the bridge. If he went for his son, the train would probably derail, fly off the bridge, and kill all the passengers on board. The engineers, the crew, and his company's customers were fully expecting him to be at his post when they passed by. Their lives were depending on it. But if he stayed in the booth and manned the rail controls, his son would drown.

In one heartrending moment, he knew what he had to do. The man turned his back to the river, gripped the rail controls, and waited the excruciatingly long two minutes for the train to pass. When it had, the man sprinted from his booth and raced down to the water's edge. His son was gone.

After a brief pause, the girl continued. "I've been told that that's what God did for me, that basically he sent his Son to die on a brutal cross so I wouldn't have to. I'm not sure I understand it all, but if that's true, if that's what God is like, then that's the God I want to believe."

That young woman said it perfectly. The cross is the symbol of the greatest act of love, the greatest act of sacrifice in history. It represents the God who moved heaven and earth to save sinners. The cross of Jesus gives us joy, not pain. It grants us freedom, not drudgery. We don't bear the cross; we rejoice in it. We don't hide it; we lift it up.

Come to Me, All You Who Are Weary and Burdened

It's time to stop apologizing for the cross. It's time to stop making excuses for our underwhelming Christian lives. It's time to stop blaming God or Christ for your bad habits, bad relationships, or bad days. And it's time to stop making the cross look like the source of all the unhappy Christians in the world.

The cross of Jesus is the greatest blessing ever given to us by a merciful and holy God. When we lift up Jesus and his cross, we actually join God in the process of drawing all humanity to himself. We appropriately point people to the life available in Christ through his work on the cross and invite them to join us in the joyous process of lifting up the cross of victory, not bearing a cross of shame and suffering.

Jesus said that his yoke was light. He took on the burdens of the world so we wouldn't have to. Walking with him—sharing his yoke—isn't trouble-free, but it's far from the life of misery that so many of his redeemed children make it out to be. Are you ready to shed your outlook of the cross being a burden, not a blessing? Are you ready to thank God for your trials, even the tough ones? Are you ready to boast in the power of the cross to transform sinners, including yourself? Are you ready to model joy in and zeal for the world's greatest symbol of hope?

Embrace Jesus and his cross. Therein is life indeed.

Small Group Discussion Questions

1. Do you own a cross—jewelry, art, a key chain? In your own words, why do you think crosses are beautiful? Have you ever thought how unusual it is that a former execution tool is now a beautiful religious symbol?

2. Have you ever felt or said that you had a cross to bear? Have you ever heard anyone else say it? What were the circumstances?

3. Read Matthew 16:24–26. Try your best to restate it in your own words and see if you can use an image other than a cross. What would be a good contemporary parallel to the cross of Jesus' day?

4. How is the invitation to take up your cross and follow Jesus a positive and not a negative one? What is good about taking up your cross?

5. Read the following verses. What do they say about the cross? List the positive attribute or benefit of the cross that Paul mentions in each.

    Romans 6:6–7
    1 Corinthians 1:17
    1 Corinthians 2:2
    Galatians 2:20
    Galatians 5:24
    Galatians 6:14
    Ephesians 2:15–16
    Philippians 3:10–11

6. What did you think about the story that the young medical technician shared with the author? What will you take away from it?

7. Read Romans 1:16. Do you think calling your hard times a cross you must bear is the same as being ashamed of the gospel? Why or why not? Have you ever been guilty of feeling ashamed of or wanting to hide your relationship with Jesus and his cross?

8. After reading this chapter, what have you learned about the cross? What are some ways you can lift it high?

9. After reading this chapter, how will you live differently?

Conclusion

Let's Trade

Well, there you have it. We've looked at some of the more common myths about grace and revealed the lies behind some of the most widely accepted misconceptions of what Jesus said. I hope you feel much emboldened and encouraged in your faith. I certainly do.

I need to point out here that Jesus doesn't simply take your burden away. He replaces it. Remember his invitation? "Take my yoke upon you and learn from me, for I am gentle and humble in heart, and you will find rest for your souls. For my yoke is easy and my burden is light" (Matt. 11:29–30). Jesus' invitation isn't for a life of completely burden-free living. As long as we live in a sinful, broken world, we will have burdens. What Jesus offers us is *his* burden. He basically says, "Hey, let's trade burdens. You give me yours, and I'll give you mine."

You're probably asking, what is Jesus' burden? What does he give us in exchange for the weight of our guilt and shame? He offers us the opportunity and responsibility of having a relationship with him. It's not burden-free, but it is burden-light. Let me list three things about what Jesus offers us (though I could list several others):

A Life of Learning

Did you notice that Jesus invited his prospective followers to learn from him? The word *disciple* actually means "learner." Jesus invited spiritual seekers to spend their lives in the exhilarating laboratory of learning from God. As the source of all eternal truth, God is eager to show us the mysteries of life, of love, of humanity, of morality, and of eternity. He is ready to instruct us and teach us in the way we should go (see Ps. 32:8). In exchange for the spiritually exhausting burdens that many of us carry, Jesus wants to give us the opportunity to sit at the feet of the Creator of the universe and to learn from him.

A Life of Loving

Another piece of the burden that goes with following Christ is the burden of love. In the same way that God was motivated by love when he sent Jesus into the world, we are called to embrace a life of love as we become yoked to him. His love becomes ours; his motives, our motives. This love flows both vertically and horizontally, as we are called to love both God and each other.

And the burden? Just how great is it? It's a burden of hungering and thirsting for God in a world where those desires can be quenched only temporarily. It's a burden of always longing for God and yet not quite being able to get enough of him. Jesus knew the same burden as he lived in full humanity. He felt the frustrations that the encumbrances of time, space, and flesh impose on a relationship with God. And yet he prevailed through those encumbrances, as will we. The blessing of this burden is that it drives us to God.

The other side of the burden is that we will care for others, and that can be heartbreaking. The call of Christ includes the assignment of not looking the other way when confronted with the pain and suffering of others, or when the ugly tentacles of injustice creep into areas that we can in fact do something about. Sharing Christ's yoke means that as he was moved to tears in the face of another's grief (see John 11:35), and as he felt compassion for the harassed, helpless, and shepherdless multitudes (see Matt. 9:36), so will we.

The burden of love is really no burden at all. For in loving others and loving God, we will experience our greatest fulfillment.

A Life of Serving

A final part of the burden of Christ's yoke is the opportunity to serve. Jesus did not come to be served but to serve, and to empty himself on behalf of others (see Phil. 2:3–11). If we are walking in his steps, we will no doubt walk into the very opportunities that he would for giving and blessing others.

Serving is the fruit of loving. The yoke of Jesus will soften our hearts and increase our compassion for those around us. But we won't stop there. Christ's yoke will move us to do something about what we see. Our burden will be the desire we have to actually lighten the load of those we see suffering from the heavy burdens of poverty, persecution, injustice, or even empty and exhausting religious rules.

Sound familiar? That's right. Jesus came to remove the heavy yoke of sin, shame, suffering, and spiritual emptiness from our weary shoulders. After he does this and gives us his gentle and light burden, he sends us out to do the same for others.

An Unlikely Blessing

I was recently in Reynosa, Mexico, on a mission trip with our church. In the week we were there, our team was blessed with the opportunity to build two small homes for two extremely impoverished families. I'd been involved with a few of these home-raisings before, so I had prepared myself for the flood of emotions—from sadness over the family's plight to the joy of being able to help them—that accompanied such a mission. But I wasn't prepared for the complete ambush of God's Spirit that I received on our last day there.

At the end of the final day, after the house was painted and nearly ready to take in its new family, we prepared for the traditional home dedication service, including prayers that God would bless the family who lived there. One of the families we had been serving lived in an old, dilapidated tin shed just several feet away from where we put their new house. On the first day I had noticed an elderly man sitting on the step of the old shed. I learned that he was the patriarch of the family, the grandfather of the woman whose family lived in the home. He had severe arthritis and was in constant pain. But on the day of the dedication, he insisted on moving the ten to fifteen feet from the old shed to his granddaughter's new home. It was gut-wrenching to watch this elderly gentleman struggle to cover the distance from one home to the other. It took him several excruciating minutes, even with the help of his family.

With the granddad now seated on the front step of the new house, we prayed and asked God's blessing on the family and their home. We encircled the house, laid hands on its walls, and prayed that God would make it holy ground. Afterward, as there was still some work and moving in to be done on the house, the grandfather needed to return to the old shed. It was more than I could take. Through a translator, I asked the man if I could help him. Before I got his response, I stepped directly in front of the man and grabbed him by his elbows. Picture two awkward seventh-graders trying to learn to dance together for the first time. That's how we looked. Suddenly I found myself just inches in front of a man I didn't know, standing face-to-face with him, walking backward very slowly as he shuffled his way forward. As we moved along, I could hear the man's grunts under his breath. He was hurting. I did all I could to lighten his load and ease his pain, but the walk was still agonizing for him.

At some point in the few moments that it took us to make our way to the old shed, the Holy Spirit spoke to me. It was an undeniable voice. He said something like, *Will, this is why you are here. This is why I made you. I want you to give your life away for the sake of lightening the load of others.* At that instant, everything in my life took on an amazing new perspective. The church I serve, the conferences I attend or speak at, the books I write, the teams I lead, my own dreams and ambitions—none of it mattered. Not when compared with the pure, simple beauty of serving a complete stranger in his time of need.

God showed me right then and there the loveliness of sharing the yoke of Jesus and of taking on his heavenly burden. It's no burden at all. God showed me that we are most like

Christ—that we are at our kingdom best—when we are serving others. That's a burden we want to bear. That's a yoke we want to share with Jesus. For in doing so, we find our highest purpose and know our greatest joy.

Free Indeed

Are you weary? It's time to bring your burden to Jesus. It's not too big, too ugly, or too entrenched for him to remove in an instant. And he will replace it with the wonderful and life-giving burden of learning, loving, and serving. Christ is more than qualified to meet all of your needs because he is God. When he promised to give you rest, he was quoting what God had said 1,400 years earlier—in other words, he was quoting himself. The God who gave the Israelites rest in their desert wanderings will give you rest in yours. So come to him. Bring him your pain, frustration, and exhaustion. He will set you free, heal you, and give you life indeed.

Appendix

You're Disqualified
Because You're Divorced

There is no such thing as a good divorce. Any time a marriage ends, even under circumstances where a divorce is the best possible and peaceable solution, the ending of a marriage is still a tragic and heartbreaking ordeal. There are no winners in divorce.

But is divorce a failure from which Christians can never recover? Does being divorced disqualify a Christian from certain forms of leadership in the church? Is someone required to never remarry if he or she is divorced? What if she didn't want the divorce? What if his wife was unfaithful? What if she was in an abusive situation? What if he was married to an unbeliever who wanted out of the marriage? What if she wasn't a Christian in her first marriage?

For many Christians, divorce is an ugly mark on their permanent record. It's like committing a Christian felony—when you lose a marriage, you lose some rights and opportunities as well.

Is that the way God sees it?

Cordel—Part 1

Cordel married his college sweetheart six months after they graduated from college. They were both believers, had volunteered with Campus Crusade for Christ, and attended the same church. Not long after they were married, Cordel started working in a hospital emergency room. It was there that he first felt a call to ministry. He wrote in his journal, "As I watched the patients come through the emergency room, I cared more for their broken souls than I did their broken bodies." His wife fully supported his change of profession, and Cordel started seminary not long thereafter. While he was there, he and his wife had two children and did their best to scrimp out a living on their modest income.

After getting his master's degree, Cordel became the pastor of a small start-up church. He was the only staff member, which meant that he and his wife took on much of the ministry load together. They also gave birth to their third child during this time. But the pressures of having three small kids in a small church took their toll. Cordel wrote, "This six-year run put a lot of pressure on our marriage."

Cordel decided that a change of venue might help matters at home. He accepted a call to a larger church, complete with a small support staff, in a different city. But the change didn't really help. Cordel's wife never really engaged in the new church, and she spent much of her spare time visiting a friend in their previous hometown. Soon Cordel's wife just quit trying. She told him, "I'm tired of the ministry and tired of being married to you." For all intents and purposes, Cordel's marriage ended then. Two months later, his wife moved out and began the divorce process. Two weeks later, Cordel resigned as pastor. He felt confused, broken, and unqualified to serve.

There's no doubt that men and women going through divorce need to have a season of reprieve to ask the hard questions about why their marriage failed. And in some cases, the minister has disqualified himself or herself from ministry, at least until he or she has been properly restored by a church (see Gal. 6:1). But does divorce really limit the ministry and church leadership options for everyone?

Was Cordel done with ministry? Should he have been? Would a leave of absence have been better than a resignation? How should his church have responded to his failing marriage?

And what about Cordel's future? What Sunday school class should he attend? Should he go to the singles' group? What if he met a strong Christian woman and fell in love? Should marriage be an option for him? Or should he be in a men's group and embrace singleness, celibacy, and nonministry for the rest of his life? Did Cordel's divorce invalidate his desire to serve in ministry? Did it invalidate the plans he believed God had for him?

The Lie

Divorce is the Christian's unpardonable sin. Once you've failed in marriage as a Christian, you're disqualified from certain options that other less damaged Christians have. You should have either chosen more wisely and married someone else or tried harder to save your marriage. But regardless, you're now a second-tier Christian. Jesus just can't have such damaged people remarrying or leading in his church.

So goes this rather brutal lie. Have you heard it? Maybe you've been on the receiving end of it, or maybe you've even voiced it about other Christians, thinking you were quoting Jesus himself. Cordel certainly thought it was true of him. Any time he was invited to teach a class or do anything else that looked like leadership in the church, he had to deal with the questions and sometimes condemnation of others before he did. He also doubted his own qualifications.

Perhaps after being told repeatedly that you're damaged goods, you start to believe it.

The Culprits

Like so many of the other things that Jesus didn't say, the source of this lie isn't God's Word but rather the misinterpretation or misapplication of it. While there are many biblical passages we could look at on this subject, three stand out most:

> "'I hate divorce,' says the LORD God of Israel, 'and I hate a man's covering himself with violence as well as with his garment,' says the LORD Almighty. So guard yourself in your spirit, and do not break faith" (Mal. 2:16).

> "Some Pharisees came to [Jesus] to test him. They asked, 'Is it lawful for a man to divorce his wife for any and every reason?'

"'Haven't you read,' he replied, 'that at the beginning the Creator "made them male and female," and said, "For this reason a man will leave his father and mother and be united to his wife, and the two will become one flesh"? So they are no longer two, but one. Therefore what God has joined together, let man not separate.'

"'Why then,' they asked, 'did Moses command that a man give his wife a certificate of divorce and send her away?'

"Jesus replied, 'Moses permitted you to divorce your wives because your hearts were hard. But it was not this way from the beginning. I tell you that anyone who divorces his wife, except for marital unfaithfulness, and marries another woman commits adultery'" (Matt. 19:3–9).

"Now the overseer must be above reproach, the husband of but one wife" (1 Tim. 3:2).

It's certainly easy to see how these verses could be used to single out divorce as a bigger sin than others or as a deal breaker for either future marriage or ministry. But I personally do not believe that such use is appropriate. Let's look briefly at each statement and see how we might indeed be misapplying it.[5]

Malachi 2:16. God hates divorce indeed. In fact, he despises it. Given the emphasis in the Bible on marriage as a metaphor for God's relationship with his people, divorce is no doubt a terrible thing in the eyes of God. But it doesn't mean that it's ultimately any more terrible than any other sin. The New Testament makes it clear that all sin is the same before God. Even though Malachi felt led to spotlight the priests' hypocrisy regarding marriage and divorce, we shouldn't conclude that God feels any more disdain for divorce than he does for murder, stealing, or prostitution. In other words, just because a sin like divorce gets prominence in a biblical passage doesn't mean it takes precedence over other equally grievous issues.

Matthew 19:3–9. The force of Jesus' words is added to only by their brevity. Jesus affirmed both God's disdain for divorce and the staying power of the seventh commandment (the prohibition against adultery). Neither had changed, either in the four hundred years since Malachi or the fourteen hundred since Moses. Both were still true. Marriage was intended to be singular and permanent—no exceptions and no escape clauses. But human sin often destroys the marriage bond, and God, by his grace, made provision for those who were victimized by their spouse.

The allowance for divorce provided for in the law of Moses was there only to protect the victim in the divorce. Jesus said that because of the hardness of our hearts, marriages would fail (see Mark 10:2–12). The divorce provision was designed to protect the rights of those (primarily women) whose spouses had abandoned or taken advantage of them.

"Except for marital unfaithfulness" isn't a permit for someone to dump their spouse if he or she no longer suits their fancy. That was precisely the type of flippant interpretation that Jesus opposed in the Pharisees. In fact, the phrase doesn't give permission to dump the spouse at all. But it does give protection and freedom to those whose spouses reject them. In such cases, Jesus was saying that a man or a woman is free to pursue another relationship if his or her spouse breaks covenant and leaves the marriage.

The bottom line is that a Christian needs to pray long and hard about leaving one marriage and creating another. Some marriage failures result despite the best efforts of one of the partners. In such cases, that partner is free to move on. There is no permanent mark on his or her record.

First Timothy 3:2. This may be the most frequently quoted verse by those who oppose a divorced man or woman being allowed to have a leadership role in the church. When talking about both elders and deacons, Paul said that church leaders had to be "the husband of but one wife." Literally, it reads "a one-woman man." It's easy to conclude that Paul meant that men who'd had serial marriages weren't qualified to lead. And that may well be what he meant. One might indeed question the leadership qualities of a person who seems to jump from one marriage to another. But what about the person Jesus referenced in Matthew 5:31–32? Is he disqualified because his spouse broke covenant with him? If Jesus didn't find sin in that man or woman's divorce and subsequent remarriage, why should his church?

One might actually conclude that Paul wasn't referencing divorce at all in his words to Timothy, and he uses similar language in his words to Titus. In both Ephesus (where Timothy was) and Crete (where Titus was), polygamy, rampant divorce and remarriage, and even temple prostitution were part of the cultural norm. In both settings, men coming to Christ were doing so from backgrounds that gave them permission to be sexually active with as many women as they wanted. With Paul's "one-woman man" phrasing, it sounds like he's rejecting the cultural practice of promiscuity, not prohibiting divorce for leaders. In fact, Paul used the word *divorce* at least three times in 1 Corinthians 7. Had Paul wanted to specify in

1 Timothy 3:2 that church leaders couldn't be divorced, why didn't he just use the word *divorce*? It sounds as if Paul had something in mind other than creating a prohibition against divorced people serving in church leadership.

The Truth

"Therefore, there is now no condemnation for those who are in Christ Jesus" (Rom. 8:1). Yes, divorce is bad, really bad. But it's no worse than anything else that Christ-followers are capable of doing. The grace afforded us by Jesus' blood is more than enough to cover all of our sins, even the sin of divorce.

To set up one's marital record as the standard by which he or she may or may not be allowed to lead in the church misses the nature of grace entirely. We know from the outset of our relationship with God that we are guilty before him. Our respective failings may be different—yours a failed marriage, mine something else. But in reality, neither of us is qualified to lead in Christ's church. If either of us leads at all, we do so by grace.

Consider some of the characters God picked out for leadership in the Bible:

Moses—he murdered an Egyptian slave master and then covered it up.

David—he committed adultery, conspiracy, and murder.

Solomon—he had over one thousand wives and concubines.

Paul—he murdered Christians and persecuted the name of Christ.

The list could be much longer. The point is that if God required a spotless past for the people he has used in history, then no one would be qualified. God, by his grace, has always chosen to use the less than perfect in his leadership initiatives. So why would the sin of divorce be any different? Is a man who had a failed marriage any guiltier than a murderer or a tax cheat? It's hard to find any biblical support for making such a distinction. Yes, divorce is a sin. Yes, it's a tragic ending of a covenant relationship. But it doesn't go on a Christian's permanent record, and it shouldn't necessarily disqualify a person from leading in Christ's church.

Exhibit A

Consider the amazing story of King David, Bathsheba, and their son Solomon. It would be hard to find a marriage that began under more scandalous circumstances. David basically forced himself on Bathsheba in an irresponsible and self-indulgent act of adulterous lust. (A woman in tenth-century BC Israel wasn't really in the position to resist the wooing of her king, even if she was married.) In the subsequent efforts to conceal his sin, David lied to and eventually ordered the death of Bathsheba's husband, Uriah. The son conceived by David and Bathsheba died as a direct result of their sin. It was one of the lowest points in Israel's history, and certainly the lowest in David's life.

But it was not the end of the story. David married Bathsheba, and she conceived again and gave birth to a son, whom they named Solomon. God sent word to them through the prophet Nathan that he had another name for their new son—Jedidiah. Jedidiah means "loved by God." Can you imagine the joy David and Bathsheba must have felt as they realized that God had decided to bless and favor their new baby? They had failed God miserably. It could have cost David his kingdom—even his life—but it didn't. God blessed David and Bathsheba's marriage and gave them a son who became arguably the greatest king in Israel's history. He was one of the wisest men in history (he gave us Proverbs, Ecclesiastes, and the Song of Solomon in the Bible), he built the Hebrew temple in Jerusalem (considered by some to be one of the Seven Wonders of the Ancient World), and he brought unprecedented peace and prosperity to Israel.

I know that David and Bathsheba don't represent a pure case of divorce and remarriage, but can you really think of a worse situation for God to bless than theirs? Yet he did. God forgave them and extended his grace to them. David didn't just remain king, but his kingdom expanded through the reign of his son Solomon. God didn't condone what David and Bathsheba did and he didn't look the other way, but he didn't write them off either. Even after their terrible marriage failure, he used them mightily.

If you're looking at a failed marriage, wondering if God can use or bless you again, I want you to draw strength, hope, and encouragement from David and Bathsheba. He blessed them; he can bless you as well.

Tom and Ronnie

Tom and Ronnie, much like David and Bathsheba, didn't get off to a good start in their marriage. They were both originally married to other people. They met through work, had an affair, divorced their respective spouses, and married each other. If they were Christians at the time, they were obviously living carnal lives.

But God didn't give up on them, and neither did he let them off the hook for their sin. Not long after their marriage, Tom and Ronnie both became very convicted that what they had done was wrong. They had one of those "Oh, dear God, what have we done?" moments. They humbled themselves before God; confessed their affair and subsequent divorces and remarriage as sin; and begged God for his mercy. Then they had to face the ugliness of the new reality they had created. How do you repent from an affair when you're now married to the person you had the affair with? Do you divorce her too and try to reconcile with your first spouse? In Tom and Ronnie's case, that wasn't possible. Neither of their first spouses wanted anything to do with them. It was as if God was saying, "You created this marriage—badly—so what are you going to do with it?"

That's when I met them. Tom and Ronnie joined the church I was leading at the time. They immediately made it a point to sit down with me and tell me their whole sordid story. They weren't asking for anything. They just wanted to be honest with me and to seek my accountability for their marriage. I must admit, I didn't want to like Tom and Ronnie and I was skeptical of them both. But I agreed to talk with them occasionally and to pray with them for their marriage.

Eventually they won me over. And Tom and Ronnie ended up having a great marriage. They took the failures of their first respective marriages, along with the pain of their own sin, and translated them into a passion for having a great marriage that honored Christ. They wanted to take what Satan had intended for evil and turn it into as much kingdom good as possible.

Tom and Ronnie also wanted to help marriages. They started a small group for couples with marriage troubles, and they helped countless couples regain their marriage momentum and have the kind of marriages that God intended.

Did we ever make Tom a deacon in the church? No. He was never really considered as a possible candidate, but not because he didn't appear qualified. Rather, we didn't want to take away from what he was doing. His ministry with Ronnie was impacting lives. God was obviously using them and blessing them.

I learned so much from Tom and Ronnie. I learned that God can and will forgive any sin. I also learned that having a spotless past—and especially a perfect marriage record—isn't required for leadership or impact in his church.

Cordel—Part 2

Two years after Cordel's wife divorced him, he met a beautiful woman at his church. They quickly started dating and were married a year later. Cordel never really thought that he shouldn't remarry. His wife had left him. From the biblical point of view, he was free to marry again. But he still was unsure about ministry. He taught an occasional Sunday school class, but even then he felt awkward about having to explain that he was divorced and remarried. It seemed the scourge of a failed marriage might never leave him.

Cordel and his wife, Christy, joined Austin Christian Fellowship ten years after they were married. I quickly saw what an amazing asset Cordel was. He was a godly man, had significant leadership and business experience, had a seminary degree, and had been a pastor. What a combination! The more I got to know Cordel, the more I liked him. So when I needed a fill-in for a weekend message, Cordel was an obvious choice.

I don't exactly remember the conversation, but when I first asked Cordel to teach for me, he brought up the fact that he was divorced. I think my response went something like this: "So?" (I've never been known for my gift of mercy or my tact.) But Cordel agreed to teach, and that was the beginning of a long ministry run for him at our church. He helped create our board of directors and led it for several years. He taught several times a year and eventually joined our staff and served as our executive pastor. Today Cordel is the leader of our discipleship ministries and supervises several staff members. He has taught on divorce and has counseled many couples through difficult marriage days.

I think God is thrilled that Cordel is serving in such a way at our church. He is a close friend and confidant to me and a committed husband, father, grandfather, and Christ-follower. And he is another great example of how God loves to restore people, even if they've been through a divorce.

Come to Me, All You Who Are Weary and Burdened

God hates divorce, but he doesn't hate divorced people. If you feel that you're damaged goods because of a failed marriage, you need to renew your mind in Christ. You've been believing a lie. Because of God's grace, divorce doesn't necessarily disqualify you from leading in God's church, having significant kingdom impact, or even remarrying.

Is it time to set aside that yoke of shame and guilt? Is it time to rethink how you see yourself and how God sees you?

Is it time for you to embrace the beautiful biblical truth that God's grace is sufficient for all your failings, even a failed marriage? Take on Jesus' yoke of forgiveness and restoration. Let his grace and mercy wash over you. Let him decide where you serve, whether or not you take a leadership position, and if you remarry. God has been surprising sinners with his outlandish grace for two thousand years. He might just surprise you too.

Notes

1. For more of Bob and Audrey's amazing story or to get some of their resources, visit their website at www.bobandaudrey.com.

2. Christine Cadena, "Unadopt a Child: The Growing Trend in Adoption Dissolutions," Associated Content, March 1, 2007, www .associatedcontent.com/article/139168/unadopt_a_child_the_grow ing_ trend_in.html?cat=25.

3. Colonel Conclusive, "Is Unadoption as Easy as Adoption?" *Blogger News Network* (blog), October 12, 2006, www.bloggernews .net/1540.

4. There are two helpful principles to remember when trying to understand the Bible, especially difficult passages. First, the Bible won't contradict itself. There are certainly places where the Bible appears at first glance to do so. But typically, with a little investigation, you'll find such perceived contradictions end up being more congruent than incongruent. If the Bible appears in one place to promise that believers can't lose their salvation, and yet in another place it appears to argue that they can, you can assume you are misreading one of the passages. They both can't be right while teaching opposite things. Keep reading and digging until one of the passages falls into perspective in light of the other.

Second, interpret difficult passages through the lens of clearer ones. There are several challenging passages in the Bible. Translational difficulties, cultural differences, and complex theological teachings make some passages hard to understand. When you stumble across such a passage, always read it in light of other, easier-to-understand sections of Scripture. Let the clear passages set the boundaries for how you interpret the unclear ones. If you have four or five passages that clearly present the same theological truth, then a passage that appears on the surface to challenge that truth needs to be read with the clear passages in mind. Since you have several passages affirming one truth, the difficult passage can't be saying something other than that. Therefore, it must be understood to be teaching something else.

You're not going to fully understand all the hard teachings in the Bible. Be content building 90 percent of your beliefs on the Scriptures that are easy to understand. God will, in time, make the other passages clear to you.

5. It is not my intention here to offer a detailed exegesis or a theological treatise of each passage, although I could. Far better minds than mine have tackled these verses from the exegetical standpoint, so I would have little new to offer. My intention here is to show these verses in the broader context of the doctrine of grace and offer a simple, alternative thought as to how they might be interpreted and applied.

Will Davis Jr. is the founding and senior pastor of Austin Christian Fellowship in Austin, Texas, and the author of several books, including the Pray Big series. Will and his wife, Susie, have three children. You can learn more about Will and follow his blog at www.willdavisjr.com.

Meet Will Davis at
www.willdavisjr.com

Read his blog, listen to his messages,
and discover his books.

Stay Connected on
Pray Big willdavisjr

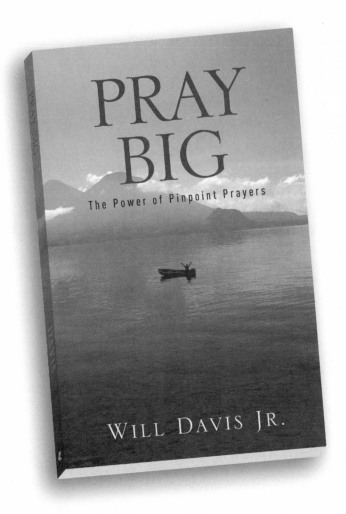

"I am alive today because of the kind of bold praying you'll find in *Pray Big*. This important book can change your expectations about prayer, challenging you to seek God much more intimately, to ask for audacious requests more boldly, and to see big answers to prayer that change lives for eternity."

—Don Piper, bestselling author, *90 Minutes in Heaven*

Revell

a division of Baker Publishing Group
www.RevellBooks.com

Available wherever books are sold.

BOLD, CONFIDENT PRAYER CAN MAKE ALL THE DIFFERENCE IN YOUR MARRIAGE AND IN YOUR FAMILY.

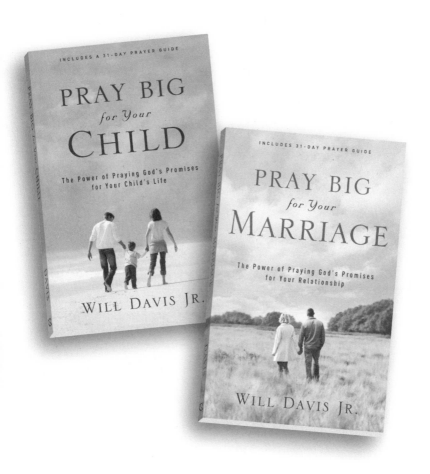

Visit www.willdavisjr.com